Bible Autobiographies And Other Bible Stories

by

Mrs. Francis E. Clark

First Fruits Press
Wilmore, Kentucky
c2015

Bible autobiographies and other Bible stories, by Mrs. Francis E. Clark.

First Fruits Press, ©2015
Previously published: Boston : United Society of Christian Endeavor, ©1921

ISBN: 9781621713333 (print), 9781621713340 (digital)

Digital version at http://place.asburyseminary.edu/christianendeavorbooks/2/

First Fruits Press is a digital imprint of the Asbury Theological Seminary, B.L. Fisher Library. Asbury Theological Seminary is the legal owner of the material previously published by the Pentecostal Publishing Co. and reserves the right to release new editions of this material as well as new material produced by Asbury Theological Seminary. Its publications are available for noncommercial and educational uses, such as research, teaching and private study. First Fruits Press has licensed the digital version of this work under the Creative Commons Attribution Noncommercial 3.0 United States License. To view a copy of this license, visit http://creativecommons.org/licenses/by-nc/3.0/us/.

For all other uses, contact:

First Fruits Press
B.L. Fisher Library
Asbury Theological Seminary
204 N. Lexington Ave.
Wilmore, KY 40390
http://place.asburyseminary.edu/firstfruits

Clark, Harriet E. (Harriet Elizabeth), 1850-
    Bible autobiographies and other Bible stories / by Mrs. Francis E. Clark ; with preface by Rev. Francis E. Clark.
    185 pages ; 21 cm.
    Wilmore, Ky. : First Fruits Press, ©2015.
    Reprint. Previously published: Boston : United Society of Christian Endeavor, ©1921.
    ISBN: 9781621713333 (pbk.)
    1. Bible – Biography. 2. Bible stories, English. I. Title.
BS551 .C6 2015

Cover design by Jonathan Ramsay

asburyseminary.edu
800.2ASBURY
204 North Lexington Avenue
Wilmore, Kentucky 40390

First Fruits Press
The Academic Open Press of Asbury Theological Seminary
204 N. Lexington Ave., Wilmore, KY 40390
859-858-2236
first.fruits@asburyseminary.edu
asbury.to/firstfruits

Bible Autobiographies
AND
Other Bible Stories

BY

MRS. FRANCIS E. CLARK

With Preface by
Rev. Francis E. Clark, D.D., LL.D.

United Society of Christian Endeavor

Boston   Chicago

Copyright, 1921
by the
UNITED SOCIETY OF CHRISTIAN ENDEAVOR

Preface

How to Use the Book

CHILDREN like to impersonate other people. They enjoy nothing better than to play that for the time being they are some one else. The little girl is mother of her doll. The boy is the big Indian, Massasoit or Samoset; and, if he can don an imitation suit of buckskin with fringes and feathers, the illusion is all the dearer to him.

If not carried too far, and if it does not involve impersonations of unworthy characters, such play and pretending are a useful part of education. Why should not this natural element to which the child takes so readily be used in the religious training of boys and girls?

This book is an attempt, and the first of its kind, so far as I know, to teach the Bible stories as autobiographies. The characters tell their own stories, and the child as he reads can easily imagine himself to be telling the story of his own life, and will become as interested in it as in the story of Jack the Giant-Killer or the adventures of Cinderella.

The book has been prepared especially with a view to the needs of mothers, Junior superintendents, Sunday-school teachers, and leaders of all kinds of children's meetings, and with the desire to enable all such leaders to make the many beautiful and touching Bible stories more vivid and graphic, and to impress them upon the child's mind as it could be done in no other way.

It will be found that almost every phase of the Christian life is here illustrated by some character who tells his story in the first person. Courage, kindness, thankfulness, generosity, prayerfulness, love, modesty, filial affection, and scores of other topics are here made concrete and level with the child's comprehension.

Any mother, teacher, or leader can by using these Bible autobiographies learn to chain the child's attention as closely as if telling a fairy story. To let a boy or girl impersonate a Bible character and tell his own story will furnish a pleasing variety in any Junior meeting or Sunday-school class. It will fix it in his memory, and will impress it upon the minds of the children as even the teacher could not do.

If the story-teller can dress in costume, it will be still more effective. A very small amount of the costumer's skill will often be all that is necessary;

PREFACE

a fez, a sash, anything unusual, would frequently answer every purpose; and, where nothing of the sort is provided, the imagination of the children will often supply all deficiencies.

Helps to make the Bible stories lively and living are still all too rare, as parents and leaders of children's meetings have often complained, and the author offers this book to her fellow workers for the children, as she tells me, with the hope and prayer that it may make their difficult but exceedingly important task easier and more delightful.

The use of the book in the home should not be forgotten. Children in the family circle like to tell stories as well as to listen to them. Then why not let the boy or girl who can read tell father and mother and brothers and sisters one of these stories as a regular Sunday-afternoon exercise or as an adjunct to Sunday family prayers? For a bedtime story no better one can be found than that of a Scripture character personified, who will teach some great truth for the child to try to practise the next day.

A few Bible word-pictures have also been added, which may be used in much the same way as the autobiographical stories.

FRANCIS E. CLARK.

CONTENTS

	PAGE
Preface	3
People Spoken of in the Stories	9
Lessons Taught by the Stories	11
The First Disobedience	13
Japheth's Story of the Rainbow	16
Abraham's Journeys	19
The Eyes of the Lord	23
Isaac the Peace-Maker	26
Jacob's Ladder	30
Miriam's Story of the Baby in the Bulrushes	33
Aaron's Story of the Golden Calf	36
The Story of Nadab and Abihu	40
Be Strong and Very Courageous	43
Samson's Story of a Strong Body and a Weak Soul	46
Ruth's Story of Daughter-Love	50
Samuel's Story of His Boyhood	54
David's Story of His Fight with a Giant	58
David's Song of the Starry Heavens	62
What the Heavens Are Telling	65
David's Story about His Son Absalom	68
The Bible That Was Lost and Found Again	71
Gehazi's Story about Coveting	74
A Story of Angel Chariots	79
A Brave Queen	83

CONTENTS

Job's Story of His Life	87
Jonah's Story about Running Away from God	90
The Shepherd's Story of the First Christmas	94
Andrew's Story of Jesus and His Friends	98
Matthew's Story of His Following Christ	102
A Sabbath Story Told by a Man with a Withered Hand	105
How to Be Great	109
A Blind Man and His Neighbors	112
A Man Who Was a Good Neighbor	117
Martha's Story of a Visit From Jesus	121
The Man Who Said, "Thank You"	124
Two Men Praying in the Temple	128
A Mother's Story about Jesus and Her Children	131
Treasures on Earth or Treasures in Heaven	135
Four Men Who Were Good Neighbors	139
Jesus in a Rich Man's Home	142
Peter's Story about Boasting	146
The Man Who Was Afraid to Do Right	149
Two Men Who Took a Walk With Jesus	153
What Happened to a Cripple	158
A Woman Who Pretended to Be Good	161
Story of Dorcas, the Friend of the Poor	164
Paul on the Damascus Road	167
A Helper of Many	171
Paul's Helpers and Hinderers	174
How Two Men "Turned the World Upside Down"	178
Timothy's Story about "Enduring Hardness"	182

Bible People Spoken of in the Stories

Name	Page
Aaron	36
Abihu	40
Abraham	19
Absalom	68
Adam	13
Ananias	161, 167, 174
Andrew	98
Angels	23, 79, 94
Babe of Bethlehem, The	94
Blind Man, A	112
Cleopas	153
David	58, 62, 65, 68
Dorcas	164
Eli	54
Elisha	74, 79
Esther	83
Eve	13
Gehazi	74
Goliath	58
Good neighbors	117, 139
Good Samaritan	117
Hagar	23
Hannah	54
Isaac	26
Ishmael	23
Israelites	36, 43, 71
Jacob	30
Japheth	16
Jesus and a blind man	112
Jesus and the children	109, 131
Jesus and the man who said, "Thank you"	124
Jesus and the man with a withered hand	105
Jesus and the man with the palsy	139
Job	87
John	98, 158
Jonah	90
Joshua	43
Josiah	71
Lame man at the Beautiful Gate, The	158
Lot	19
Martha and Mary	121
Matthew	102
Miriam	33
Mordecai	83
Moses	33, 36
Naaman	74
Nadab	40
Naomi	50
Noah	16
Palsy, The man with the	139
Paul	167, 171, 174, 178, 182
Peter	109, 146, 158, 164
Pharisee and the publican, The	128
Philistines	26, 46, 58
Phœbe	171, 174
Pilate	149
Publicans	102, 128, 142
Rich young ruler, The	135
Ruth	50
Samaritan, The Good	117
Samson	46
Samuel	54
Sapphira	161
Silas	178
"Thank you," The man who said	124
Timothy	182
Withered hand, The man with a	105
Zacchæus	142

Lessons Taught by the Stories

	PAGE
Abide with me	153
Afraid to do right,	36, 149
Angel helpers	23, 79, 94
Answer to prayer, An	54
Atoning for wrongdoing	142
Being or seeming	161
Bible, The lost	71
Blind man, Jesus and a,	112
Boasting	128, 146
Brave queen, A	83
Bringing others to Christ	98, 139, 178
Caring for the poor,	87, 164
Children, Jesus and,	109, 131
Christ, Confessing	167
Christ, The risen	153
Christmas	94
Christ's friends	98, 121
Confessing Christ	167
Courage and trust,	43, 58, 79, 83
Covenants	16, 30, 71
Covetousness	74
Cowardice	36, 149
Daughter-love	50
Disciples	98, 102
Disobeying God	13, 40
Doing God's errands	54
Doing good	164, 171

	PAGE
Easter	153
Enduring hardness	182
Eyes open	79
Faith	105, 139, 158
Father-love	68
Fear of others	36
Feast of Purim	83
Fighting a giant	58
Following Christ	98, 102
Friends of Christ	98, 121
Friendship with God	19
Generosity	87
Giant, Fighting a	58
Giving what we can,	87, 158, 164
God sees us	23
God with us	23, 30
God's call	102
God's care for us	58
God's house	30
God's laws	71
God's little messenger	54
God's promises	16
Greatness, True	109
Growing in grace	54
Heavens, The starry,	62, 65
Helping	164, 171, 174
Heroism	83
Hiding from God	13, 90
Hindering	174

LESSONS TAUGHT BY THE STORIES

	Page		Page
Home, Jesus in the,	121, 142	Open eyes	79
Honoring parents	50	Parents, Honoring	50
How to be unhappy,	13, 30, 74	Peace-making	26
		Poor, Caring for the,	87, 164
How to pray	128	Praising God	158
How to show our love to Christ	121	Prayer	54, 128
		Praying and watching	33
Humility	109	Pretending to be good,	161
Hypocrisy	161	Promises, God's	16
Idols	19, 178	Psalm 8	62
Irreverence	40	Psalm 19	65
Jesus and a blind man	112	Purim, The feast of	83
Jesus and the children,	109, 131	Quarrelling	26
		Queen, A brave	83
Jesus and the Sabbath,	105, 112	Rainbow, The	16
		Repentance	146
Jesus in the home	121, 142	Resurrection	153
Jesus, Walking with	153	Riches	74, 135
Jesus, Wanting to see	142	Running away from God	90
Joy to the world	94		
Kindness	117	Sabbath-keeping	105, 112
Kindness to the poor,	87, 164	Saying, "Thank you,"	124, 158
Led astray by others	36		
Lending to the Lord	87	Selfishness	30, 68, 74
Lord is my shepherd, The	58	Shepherd, The Lord is my	58
		Shirking duty	90
Lost Bible, The	71	Sister-love	33
Love of money	74, 135	Song of the starry heavens	62, 65
Love to Christ, How to show our	121		
		Song of the sun	65
Loving our neighbors,	117, 139, 164	Sorrow for sin	146
		Starry heavens, The	62, 65
Lying	74, 161	Strength of body or soul,	46
Making the world better,	178	Strong and yet weak	46
Missionaries, Two	178	Sun, The	65
Missionary, An unwilling,	90	Temperance	40
Money, Love of	74, 135	Thankfulness	124, 158
Mothers and daughters,	50	Thou God seest me	23
Neighbors	117, 139, 164		

12 LESSONS TAUGHT BY THE STORIES

	PAGE
Treasures on earth or in heaven	135
True greatness	109
Trust	43, 58, 79, 83
Turning the world upside down	178
Unhappy, How to be,	13, 30, 74
Walking with Jesus	153
Wanting to see Jesus	142
Welcoming Jesus to the home	121, 142
What the heavens are telling	65
What to be afraid of	36
Wrong-doing, Atoning for	142

THE FIRST DISOBEDIENCE

(As Eve might tell the story if she could come back)

WE were alone in the world, and we lived in a beautiful garden that God Himself had prepared for us. It was a wonderful garden, with all kinds of trees and flowers and fruits; for out of the ground the Lord had made to grow "every tree that is pleasant to the sight and good for food."

All these good and beautiful things were for us to take care of and to enjoy; and God had given us just one law, to test us and see whether we would choose to obey Him. We might eat the fruit of every tree in the garden except one, the "tree of knowledge of good and evil." That was forbidden.

We were very happy in our beautiful garden until Satan tempted me to disobey God. I was walking one day near the tree of knowledge, thinking how beautiful a tree it was, and how nice the fruit looked; and Satan put the thought into my mind that I should taste it, just as he sometimes puts wrong thoughts into your minds, and tempts you to do what you know is wrong. I knew that I ought to obey God, and that it would be better to turn away from the tree at once; but instead of doing that I stayed there, admiring the tree, and smelling of the fruit, and longing for it until I felt as though I must just taste it. Instead of crowding out wrong thoughts with right thoughts I yielded to the temptation, and persuaded myself that it could not be any great harm just to taste the fruit. And so I ate some of the forbidden fruit; and then I gave some of it to Adam and led him to disobey God too.

I had thought I should be happier to do what I wanted to, but I soon found, as everybody finds who tries it, that doing what *I* pleased, whether it pleased God or not, only made me unhappy. As soon as I had disobeyed I began to be afraid and ashamed. We neither of us wanted God to know what we had done; so we went and hid ourselves in the garden. But we could not hide away from God, and we could not be happy while we were disobeying Him. God called us, and we had to confess our sin. We were sent away from our beautiful garden; and, though we were more and more sorry and ashamed when we saw how our sin looked to God, we could never go back there again, and we could never even think of the garden without unhappiness, remembering our disobedience to God who had been so good to us.

THE FIRST DISOBEDIENCE 15

Always after that we knew that we can be truly happy only when we obey God, and our greatest punishment was the memory of our disobedience to our Father in heaven. If I could live my life over again, I would say to God

"With my whole heart will I seek thee;
O let me not wander from thy commandments."

THE STORY OF THE RAINBOW

(*As Japheth might have told it*)

I was one of Noah's sons, and I had been in the ark with all of our family during all those long days when the flood was upon the earth. We had lived in a wicked world, and I had often heard my father talking with the neighbors about loving God and serving Him; but no one cared for his preaching, and many scoffed and made fun when he began to build the ark. What was the use, they asked, of building that great big boat on the dry land? What would he ever do with it when it was finished?

However, we did finish it at last, though it had taken a long, long time. Then we all went in, and God shut the door. The flood came, and all the scoffing people were drowned, and we only were alive; and "the waters prevailed upon the earth a hundred and fifty days." It seemed a long, long time to us; and often I used to wonder whether the water would ever dry up.

Can you imagine how glad we were when at last we saw the dry land again? O, you cannot think

THE STORY OF THE RAINBOW 17

how beautiful the world looked to us. The grass was so green, and the sky was so blue, and it seemed so wonderful to look at the trees again and the beautiful flowers!

The very first thing that Noah, my father, did was to build an altar, which was to us what your church is to you; and there we worshipped God, and thanked Him for taking care of us and for giving back to us so beautiful a world. Then the Lord made this wonderful promise to Noah: "I will not again smite any more everything living, as I have done."

We were all very happy in believing God's wonderful promise; but one day not long after that it began to rain, and some of us were almost afraid we were going to have another flood, though we had God's promise that it should never be so again. But the shower lasted only a little while, and then we saw in the sky the most beautiful rainbow that I had ever seen. And God said: "I do set my bow in the cloud, and it shall be for a token of a covenant between me and the earth. And it shall come to pass, when I bring a cloud over the earth, that the bow shall be seen in the cloud; and I will remember my covenant."

Of course we had often seen a rainbow before, though it had never had any special meaning for us; but from this time we could never look at a rainbow without thinking of God's covenant, for He had said it was to be a sign to us that God would keep His promise. I believe God would be pleased if every time we see a rainbow we should say to ourselves, "This is a beautiful sign for us; we must always remember, God will keep His promises."

A STORY ABOUT ABRAHAM

(The man who was called "The Friend of God")

THERE was once a young man who lived far away across the seas, in a city called Ur. The people all around him were heathen who knew nothing about the true God, but built idol temples, and worshipped gods that they made themselves; some one who lived long afterwards, and who felt much as Abraham must have felt, wrote this about their gods:

> "Their idols are silver and gold,
> The work of men's hands.
> They have mouths, but they speak not;
> Eyes have they, but they see not;
> They have ears, but they hear not;
> Noses have they, but they smell not;
> They have hands, but they handle not;
> Feet have they, but they walk not;
> Neither speak they through their throat."

Abraham was only a young man, but he felt that his people were wrong and that such gods as those could do nothing for them; and he would not worship in their temples or pray to their idol gods.

He believed that there must be a greater One who had made the earth and all things therein, and to Him he prayed.

One day this young man went to his father, and I think he probably said something like this: "Father, let us go away from this place, where the people worship idols and are trying to make us do the same. I believe that the true God calls us to go away to another country where we can worship Him and teach others to do so too."

We do not know that he said just these words, or just how God's call came to him; but in some way the message had come, and we are told that "by faith, Abraham, when he was called, . . . obeyed; and he went out, not knowing whither he went."

If you and I could have been there then, we might have seen one day a little company of people moving out of the city of Ur, with all their belongings. There were Abraham, and his father, and his wife; and there was Lot, Abraham's nephew; and there were, I suppose, a good many of their servants and their cattle, for they had great possessions; and together they travelled till they came to the city of Haran, a long way from Ur. There they stopped and settled down for a time, perhaps because Terah, Abraham's father, was too tired to

A STORY ABOUT ABRAHAM 21

travel further. They lived there in Haran for several years, until Terah died in a good old age; and then Abraham felt that God called him to go away into another country; so he and his wife, and Lot, his nephew, with their servants, and their cattle, and their flocks, journeyed on till they came to Shechem in the land of Canaan; and there Abraham built an altar, and there he prayed to God, and there he listened to God's voice; and that altar meant to him just what our church means to us, a place to worship God.

Afterward Abraham moved many times, to different places in the land of Canaan; but wherever he settled down to live for a while there he always built an altar, until by and by there were altars all over the land of Canaan. I feel sure that often the heathen people around him would ask him what those altars were for, and Abraham would tell them of the "living God who made the heaven and the earth." I cannot help thinking that through Abraham's words and through his life of faith and obedience some of those people must have learned to worship the true God as Abraham did.

The Bible tells us a good many other stories about Abraham, and in these stories we learn that because he believed God's promises and obeyed

God's commands a New Testament writer could afterward say of him, "Abraham believed God, and it was reckoned unto him for righteousness, and he was called the friend of God." I believe that, if we live such lives of faith and obedience as Abraham's, we too may sometime be called "friends of God," for Jesus Himself has said,

"Ye are my friends, if ye do whatsoever I command you."

"THE EYES OF THE LORD ARE IN EVERY PLACE"

"Thou God seest me"

(As Hagar might tell the story)

I was an Egyptian girl who lived long, long ago, and my name was Hagar. I had lived in Egypt through all my girlhood, until I was given as a handmaid to a Hebrew woman named Sarah, who had been visiting in my country with Abraham, her husband.

I found my life with her hard in many ways, and I did not like my mistress; but I know that I was sometimes very rude and ill-natured, and perhaps it is no wonder that she was often very cross to me, and scolded me more than I thought I deserved. One day, after my mistress had been unusually severe with me, I felt that she was very unjust, and it seemed as though I could not bear it another minute; so I ran away from what I thought was a hard place, and soon found myself in a harder one.

God could see me all the time, and He knew

that it was hard for me; but He wanted me to bear it a little while longer, because it would be better for me in the end. I had learned something about God in my Hebrew home, but I did not know then that God could see me always, and would surely help me if I would trust Him.

I wandered off without knowing where I was going, until I found myself in the desert, far away from my cruel mistress and free to do just what I pleased.

I was standing alone and forlorn in the wilderness, near a beautiful fountain which I had discovered; but the eyes of the Lord were upon me all the time, and God sent an angel to bring me a message. I must go back, the angel said, to the place where God had put me, and must bear my trials and troubles a little longer. Sometime, he said, I should be very happy, for God would give me a little son, and I must call his name Ishmael, which means "God hears"; and so my little son's very name would be a reminder to me of God's care for me.

The angel's message made me very happy, and I was always very glad to remember the promise God had made about Ishmael; but, after all, the one thing that I oftenest remembered when I thought of that day in the desert alone with God was not the blessing God had promised, nor even the command to go back again to my cruel mistress and bear my troubles patiently; it was the thought that God had seen me all the time, and that He had seen me all my life.

I called the well by a name that you might find hard to pronounce, but it meant a great deal to me, for it helped me to remember God. I called it Beer-lahai-roi, and that means "the well of the living one that seeth me."

I always loved that place, and in after-years I used to go there sometimes to think about the God who sees me always; and, though I often felt in other places and at other times that the eyes of the Lord were upon me, yet He always seemed a little nearer to me there; and often when I was in trouble or sorrow I would think of Beer-lahai-roi, and would say to myself, "Thou God seest me!" and that thought always helped me.

ISAAC THE PEACE-MAKER

(*A Word Picture*)

If you and I had been living hundreds and hundreds of years ago we might have seen in a country far across the seas a family of four people living in tents, a father and mother and two sons. The man was very rich, and was known to everybody in that country as a great man, for he had "possessions of flocks, and possessions of herds, and a great household." Indeed, he grew so very rich and prosperous that the people of that land envied him and tried to injure him.

Now, because he had so many flocks and herds his most important possession was a great well which his father Abraham had dug many years before; for in that country water was often very scarce, and a good well was very valuable. The Philistines, who were his enemies, came against him, and filled up all the wells that he had, and said to him, "You must go away from here; we don't want you to get stronger and more powerful than we are."

ISAAC THE PEACE-MAKER 27

If we had been there then, I think we should have seen Isaac's servants coming to him very indignantly, and telling him how mean a thing those Philistines had done, and that the only thing to do would be for all the men to go out and fight them. "We'll teach them that they can't treat us like that," they would say.

If Isaac had been like some men, he would have agreed to this plan at once; and there would have been war between him and his neighbors, and many people would have been killed, and one side or the other would have won, and there would have been hate and cruelty on both sides.

I suppose that Isaac thought of all this, and I think he felt that there could never be any possessions anywhere that were worth so much awful cruelty and hate and murder. So he quietly moved himself and his possessions away to another place, and dug again the wells that they had dug in the days of Abraham. We might have heard his servants grumbling a little among themselves, and then saying, "Well, perhaps his way is best, and we had better be living and digging wells here than dead and dying there in the fields"; and I think they must have felt glad that they themselves had not killed any one. They must have been a happy company when they had finished digging new wells, and they called them the same names that Abraham had called them long ago.

But even here they were not allowed to live in peace, for the Philistines came again, and this time we might have seen Isaac's servants fighting with them for the possession of the best well of all. We should have seen their faces grow more and more angry as the fighting went on, but Isaac soon stopped it, saying, "I think we must call this the 'Well of Quarrelling'; we will move away and let them have it." So they moved further away, and dug another well.

Again the Philistines came out against them, and we might have heard the herdsmen saying to Isaac: "It is enough! There is such a thing as being too peaceable; those men will think you are afraid of them; you *must* let us fight them now." I can imagine Isaac saying quietly: "What difference does it make what they *think? We know* that we are not afraid. I have no doubt that we could beat them, but I will not have the blood of these men on my hands. We can dig other wells. Let us have peace." And then he said, "We will call this the 'Well of Hatred,' because it has caused such angry feelings. There is surely room enough for us all somewhere without fighting."

Isaac's words proved true; for this time the

Philistines left him in peace, and he called the new well "Room-enough Well," "for now," he says, "the Lord hath made room for us."

Was not that much better than hatred and fighting and murder? I do not believe a man like Isaac could ever have enjoyed a well that he had won by fighting. But now he had a happy home with his family, and he felt that the Lord Himself had made room for him, and he could enjoy it in peace. And he built an altar, and called upon the name of the Lord. And so Isaac many hundreds of years ago learned the same lesson which Paul many years afterward tried to teach the Christians in Rome, and which we all need to learn to-day,

"If it be possible, as much as in you lieth, be at peace with all men."

JACOB'S LADDER

(A story of the man who did not know God was with him)

THERE was once a man who had been doing very wrong. He had cheated his own brother, and had lied to his aged father; and now he was running away from the angry brother, who had threatened to kill him. All day long he hurried on, getting farther and farther from his home; and I suppose he must have felt very homesick and lonely, for he was going to a far country, and he was all alone. I don't know whether he was really sorry for the wrong he had done, or only afraid he would be punished for doing it. I think he must have thought sometimes, as he hurried along, of the poor old father he had deceived, and of the angry brother he had wronged; but I am afraid he was not thinking much about God.

At last it began to grow dark, and he looked for a place to sleep. There were no houses near, and he must have felt more lonesome than ever. He was in a very lonely place, with high, rocky cliffs around him; and he had to lie down to sleep on the

JACOB'S LADDER

ground, with a stone for his pillow. I don't believe that even then he was thinking about God, but God was thinking about him, a lonely, sinful man, and waiting to draw near to him.

That night he had a wonderful dream about angels going up and down a ladder that reached from earth to heaven; and at the top of the ladder he thought he saw God! Then, as he lay there alone in the darkness, God whispered a wonderful message to him: "I am with thee, and will keep thee in all places whither thou goest, and will bring thee again into this land."

Then, very suddenly, I think, Jacob waked from his sleep, and it seemed to him that God was very near him. "Surely the Lord is in this lonely place," he said, "and I did not know it." And then I think he himself drew near to God as he made some solemn promises. He took his stone pillow to be a stone pillar, and, setting it up as a little monument, he anointed it with oil, which was his way of saying, "This is a holy pillar." Then he said, "The name of this place shall be Bethel, for that means 'God's house.'" And then he made a promise to God: "If the Lord will be with me, as He has promised," he said, "then the Lord shall always be my God, and of all that He shall give me, I will surely give a tenth back to Him; and this stone pillow which I have set up for a pillar shall be God's house.''

Many years later he came back to Bethel again, and built an altar to God, and worshipped Him there; for he had learned now that God was near to him, and that he could draw near to God in prayer. I think this story has been kept for us through all these years that we may know that God often draws very near to us, even when we do not know it, and He is always waiting to bless us whenever we draw near to Him in **prayer.**

STORY OF MIRIAM, THE KIND SISTER

(*As she herself might tell it*)

My father and mother were Israelites in Egypt at the time of the cruel bondage of our people. I had one little brother named Aaron, who was nearly three years old when the wicked king made a decree that every little boy who should be born in an Israelite home should be killed. After that every home into which a little boy was born was soon made into a house of mourning.

When God sent a little baby boy into our own home, my mother was very anxious; and, when she first let me see him, she said to me, "Sh! do not tell any one; if they hear about it, the cruel soldiers will kill him."

Every day mother and I watched over my new little brother, trying to keep him so carefully hidden away that no one should know we had a baby in our home. Very often we prayed that God would not let him be killed, and always we were trying to plan some way of keeping him hidden.

At last mother thought of a plan, and I think it was God that gave her the thought. She made a little covered basket of bulrushes, and made it water-tight, and put in a soft lining; and then one morning, very early, we carried our baby to the river, and put him into the little basket; then we both prayed, and mother kissed him, and left me to watch over him. She thought that if she stayed people would suspect that she was his mother, but no one would pay any attention to a little girl who seemed to be playing by the river.

I was afraid, though; I was almost tempted to run away, for I thought, if the cruel soldiers should come, perhaps they would throw us both into the river; but I was determined that no one should hurt my little brother if I could help it; so I just prayed, and watched, and tried to think what to do.

At last, while I was praying and watching, the king's daughter came down to the river to bathe, and at once she noticed the little basket, and sent a maid to bring it to her, that she might see what was in it; and all the time I was praying that she might be kind to my little brother.

When she opened it, and the baby saw strange faces all around him, he cried; and the princess looked down so kindly and lovingly on his little face that I took courage and went towards her; when I heard her say, "This must be a little He-

STORY OF MIRIAM, THE KIND SISTER 35

brew baby," I said, "Shall I go and call a nurse of the Hebrew women, that she may nurse the child for you?" That idea seemed to please the princess, and she looked at me, and said, "Go." You may be sure that I went as quickly as possible, and brought mother, for she was not very far away.

Then the princess said, "Take this child, and nurse it for me, and I will give you your wages."

So we took the baby back home again with joy in our hearts, and mother and I took care of him till he was big enough to go to the palace. After that we did not see him very often until many years later; but we always prayed for him, and God took care of him in the palace, and many years later God let me go with him when he led our people out of Egypt.

But I often used to wonder what would have happened if I had not been faithful to my trust and had not taken good care of my little brother. God could have kept him safe in some other way without my help, but I should have lost the chance of doing my part. I think all girls ought to be very good to their brothers and sisters, and help them, and pray for them always.

AARON'S STORY OF THE GOLDEN CALF

I was born a slave in the land of Egypt, and I lived there as a slave until I was an old man. Perhaps it was partly because I had been a slave for so many years that I was so easily led to do wrong afterward. That was no excuse for me, though; for I had a good father and mother, and they had taught me to fear God and keep His commandments, and I knew that I ought to have been more afraid of grieving God than of displeasing my own people.

When King Pharaoh began to fear that there might sometime be too many of us Hebrews in the land of Egypt, he issued a cruel edict that all the little baby boys in the Hebrew families should be thrown into the river as soon as they were born. But my father and mother had learned to trust and not be afraid, and it is written of them in the Bible that "they were not afraid of the king's commandment." O, how I wish I had always been as brave as they were!

When my little brother Moses was born, my

mother prayed; and God helped her to plan a way by which not only was his life saved, but he was brought up in the king's palace, and was taught "all the wisdom of the Egyptians."

God had planned that Moses and I should lead our people out of Egypt, but it was not until we were old men that He called us to do it. The Egyptians all around us worshipped false gods, but our people had always been taught to worship the true God, and through His help Moses was able to do great wonders in the land of Egypt; and God led us out in safety. King Pharaoh and his horsemen followed us, but God destroyed them in the Red Sea.

We journeyed in the wilderness to Mt. Sinai, and then God called Moses up into the mountain, that he might be there alone with his God, and learn God's laws for His people. Moses was so long away that some of the people thought he would never come back, and they began to be afraid, and urged me to make them a god like the Egyptian gods. "Make us gods," they said, "which shall go before us; for as for this Moses, the man that brought us up out of the land of Egypt, we don't know what has become of him."

Of course I knew that they were wrong and were trying to make me do wrong, but I was afraid.

They were so many, and I was just one! What could I do against all those people, when they were so determined to have a god that they could see? They were afraid to journey on without a god to lead them, and so their fear led them to sin; I was afraid of them, and so my fear led me to sin too. Oh, I have always felt so sorry and ashamed to think that my name has gone down through all the ages as the man who was afraid to do right! Why, what could those people have done to me? They could only have killed me at the worst, and I don't believe now that they would have done that. I think they would have been afraid to do it, because I was their leader next to Moses. But even if they had killed me, I should have gone joyfully to my God, knowing that I was trying to do His will.

But I was afraid; and so I did what they asked, and made them a golden calf such as they had seen in Egypt; and they danced around it and worshipped it, and I stood looking on.

Oh, how ashamed I was when Moses came down to give us God's ten laws, and saw what we were doing! Though I was not worshipping the golden calf, yet I felt that I was more to blame than my people; for I had made the calf, and allowed them to worship it.

I tried to stammer out some lame excuses to

Moses, but the only thing that I could say for myself was that I was afraid of the people, and I knew that God would not accept that excuse.

Afterward I tried to show that I had truly repented, and I tried to serve God faithfully; but I could never undo what I had done, and the thought of it always made me unhappy, even though I believe that God forgave it. I know now that what the wise man afterward wrote is surely true,

"The fear of man bringeth a snare, but whoso putteth his trust in the Lord shall be safe."

THE STORY OF NADAB AND ABIHU

(A Temperance Story)

God had told the Israelites how to build a house for Him, and how to worship Him there. He had said that as a part of their worship the priest should burn sweet incense before the Lord every morning upon the golden altar. One day a very sad thing happened. Two of Aaron's sons, whom God had specially appointed to be priests, disobeyed God. The Bible tells us that they "offered strange fire before the Lord, which he commanded them not."

God had given them very definite directions about the incense that should be used, and how it should be made, and about the fire with which it should be burned; and they did exactly what He had told them they must not do, and even did it as a part of their worship. What a terrible mockery it was, to pretend to be worshipping God, when they were really disobeying Him! And yet have we not sometimes done something very much like that? God does not care for our worship

THE STORY OF NADAB AND ABIHU 41

while we are disobeying Him. We need to watch ourselves while we blame these others.

This was such open disobedience that it could not be excused. God had said, "I will be sanctified in them that come nigh me"; and they had not sanctified Him, but were dishonoring Him; and God sent down fire from heaven and destroyed them.

Then God said to Aaron, "Do not drink wine nor strong drink, thou, nor thy sons with thee, when ye go into the tabernacle of the congregation, lest ye die, . . . that ye may put difference between holy and unholy, and between unclean and clean." Because God said this to Aaron we think that probably Nadab and his brother had been drinking, and so did not realize what they were doing. Is it not very wicked as well as foolish for a man to do what he knows will put him into such a condition that he is not responsible for what he is doing? And yet even now people take strong drink, when they know that they will be very likely to get into such a condition as that. We say, "They were not themselves." But they might have been themselves. It is their own fault that they are not themselves.

How would you feel if you knew that some day you would not be yourself, but a very different person, perhaps a ragged, dirty, staggering, quarrelsome person? Would you choose to make yourself into that kind of person? And yet there are many people who drink what they know may cause just such a change as that.

There are many lessons that we might learn from this story of the two priests who disobeyed God; but to-day we are going to remember just this one thing, that it was strong drink that caused their sin, and we must all do all we can to put down this great evil in the world, and to work for temperance, and right living, and obedience to God.

BE STRONG AND VERY COURAGEOUS

(A story that Joshua might have told)

WHEN I was chosen to take Moses' place as leader of a great people, it seemed to me almost too heavy a responsibility. But Moses had chosen me, and God had chosen me; and I was ever one to go forward, and at least attempt whatever was given me to do. And yet my heart almost failed me. How could all this great company of many thousands of men, women, and children cross the swiftly flowing river Jordan? And how should we conquer all those heathen nations? I had forgotten the Anakim, the giants, and how forty years ago the ten spies who went with Caleb and me to spy out the land had said that we were only like grasshoppers before them. But then I remembered that God had promised to be with the "grasshoppers"; and I resolved to do my best, though the work was very great, and looked to me almost impossible.

But God knew that my heart was discouraged, and He Himself spoke to me, and gave me His own promise that, as He had been with Moses, so He would be with me, *"Only be thou strong and very courageous!*" And so I took God's own words to me, to be my watchword in all the future days. And I learned that to go bravely forward, trusting in God, was the surest way to win the victory.

And now, as we camped on the shores of the Jordan, I said to the people, "Consecrate yourselves, for to-morrow the Lord will do wonders among you." I wanted them all to find courage in remembering that God was very near us, and that *He* was really their leader, not I. Then I directed that the priests should go first, carrying the ark, and that they should walk out into the river, and stand near it. They carried the same ark of the covenant that we had made in the wilderness according to God's directions; and we held it very sacred, for it was the symbol of God's presence among us, just as God's house is that to you to-day.

I knew what God had promised, but it took great courage to trust His promise and act upon it; but God helped me, and I gave out the orders, and we all marched down to the brink of the river. Very anxiously I watched as the priests walked down into the swift current. Would a way really be opened for us through the waters as God had said? As I watched, I saw the waters above us stand still, and form a sort of wall to protect us, and the waters below flowed on until a way was made for us; and we all walked over through the dry bed of the river, just as God had promised.

I do not know even now just how God worked that miracle for us, whether He sent a strong wind that drove back the waters, whether perhaps some obstacle above, sent by Him, stopped the flowing of the river, or whether He simply spoke the word, and the waters stayed at His bidding. I only know that in some way God Himself opened a path for us to pass through the river, just as He had promised. And so our faith was strengthened, and our courage increased, and we learned to be "strong in the Lord," for that is the only way to be truly strong and courageous; and we know that we may always trust His promises, for

"No word He hath spoken
Was ever yet broken."

A MAN WITH A STRONG BODY AND A WEAK SOUL

(As Samson might tell the story if he could come back)

I WAS a man who ought to have been strong in the Lord, for God had given me a good father and mother, who had prayed for me, and had asked counsel of God that they might know how to train me and guide me aright. "How shall we order the child, and how shall we do unto him?" was their prayer. They had tried to teach me the way of the Lord even from a little child, and long ago it was written of me, "And the child grew, and the Lord blessed him," and God had promised that I should "begin to deliver Israel out of the hand of the Philistines."

God had given me a very strong body, too, and that was meant to be a help to me in the work that God wanted me to do. Long before I was born my people had been led by Joshua into the land that God had promised to them; but they had many enemies, and in my time our worst and strongest enemies were the Philistines; and I knew

STRONG BODY AND WEAK SOUL 47

that God had promised that I should begin to deliver my people from their power.

I did *begin* to deliver them, and by the great strength that God had given me and with God's help I did much to free my people from their power, but I might have done much more. For twenty years I was a judge in Israel, and the Philistines were much afraid of me because I was so very strong and not afraid of anything; and they were always trying to catch me and either kill me or put me in prison.

I was once in one of their cities, and they locked the great heavy city gates, so that I could not get out in the night; and they said that in the morning when the gates were opened they would kill me as I went out. But I went out in the middle of the night in spite of their shutting the big city gates; you will find the whole story written in the Bible, and you will read that I "took the doors of the gate of the city, and the two posts, and went away with them, bar and all." I should like to have seen their faces when they went to open the gates in the morning. I carried the gates and posts and bar and everything up to the top of a hill, and left them there for the people to take whenever they could find men strong enough to carry them back. You will find in the Bible other stories about my great strong body, but you will not find anything about a strong soul.

Sometimes I think my soul was stronger when I was a little child than it was after I became a man, because then I chose to go my own way, whether it was God's way or not. I just wanted to have a good time without thinking much about God; and so, though my body grew strong, my soul grew weak. It is always so when we just choose to seek for pleasure and good times and forget God. It is only when we are trying every day to please God that souls grow strong; and every time that we disobey God, and do those things that we ought not to do, our souls grow smaller and weaker. I followed my own way so much, and wandered so far from God's way, that my soul grew pretty small and weak, and at last I had such a little bit of a soul, and such a poor, weak will, that I did a very foolish thing. I let myself be persuaded to tell a Philistine woman wherein my great strength lay.

God had said that I should always let my hair grow long, and that should be a sign of my obedience to Him; and I knew that I ought not to tell the secret, and yet I did tell it. Of course the woman told my enemies; she had teased the secret out of me for that very purpose, and I was not strong enough in soul to resist the teasing. The Philistines, who had been watching for a chance to overpower me, came upon me while I was asleep, and cut my hair, and God took away the great strength which I had not used wisely, and then I became weak as other men. They shut me up in a prison, and put out my eyes; and then, as a poor, blind prisoner I had to work for them, and often they used to come and mock me and make fun of me as I was grinding in the prison-house every day.

And so I lost the great opportunity that had been given to me to be a strong power for God in my country. In the prison I repented of my sins, and told God how sorry I was for the life I had lived and the strength I had wasted; and God forgave me, and gave me back my strength, though I was never able to see again, for God did not give me back my two eyes; yet I was able to destroy a great many of my country's enemies before I died, and you can read the story of how I did it in the Bible.

My story is just the story of wasted opportunities. If I could live my life over again, I would "seek the Lord and his strength," and I would take for my motto the words that the wise man wrote long years afterward,

"The way of the Lord is strength."

A STORY OF DAUGHTER-LOVE

(*As Ruth herself might have told it*)

I WAS born in the land of Moab, in a heathen country, and all my relations and all my neighbors worshipped idols. We always felt that the gods were angry with us, and we thought they would surely do us harm unless we brought them many gifts and offerings to appease them. It was not a happy religion, but it was the only religion I knew. But, when I went to live in the home of Naomi, I learned a better way; for she taught me that her God was a God of love, and I often used to join in her worship.

Naomi was so kind and loving a mother to Orpah and me that we were very happy in her home; and, when she decided to go back to her own country, I quickly decided to go with her. Naomi tried to persuade me to stay with my own people, for she thought I should be lonesome and unhappy in a strange land among strange people; but my mind was fully made up, and I said, "Do not ask me to leave thee, for where thou goest I will go; thy people shall be my people, and thy God my God." When she saw that I was determined to go with her, she no longer tried to persuade me, and, kissing my sister-in-law Orpah good-by, we two went on until we came to Bethlehem, Naomi's old home.

Her friends gave her a kindly welcome, for she was so good a woman that every one seemed to love her; and we soon made a happy home for ourselves, even though we were poor. Then I told Naomi that I wanted to go into the fields and glean after the reapers; for it was now just the harvest-time, and I wanted to earn a living for both of us; and she said, "Go, my daughter." Then I joyfully went out and gleaned in the fields, and the Lord led me to the field of a very kind man, who said that I might go every day and glean after his reapers; and I learned afterward, though I did not know it then, that he had said to them, "Let her glean even among the sheaves, and reproach her not; and let fall also some of the handfuls of purpose for her, and leave them that she may glean them."

When I tried to thank him for his kindness, he said, "I have heard of all your kindness to your mother-in-law, and how you have left your own father and mother and your home, and have come here to a strange land, and are trying to take care of your mother-in-law; may you have a full reward from the God of Israel, under whose wings you are come to trust."

And so Naomi and I lived together in the land of Israel, and every day I worked for her, and loved her, and tried to make her happy; and by and by God gave me a happy home of my own, and Naomi lived with me. She taught me the Ten Commandments that God gave to her people through Moses, and I tried to obey them; but I always especially loved the one that afterward was called "the first commandment with promise:"

"Honor thy father and thy mother, that thy days may be long upon the land which the Lord thy God giveth thee."

NAOMI AND RUTH

"Entreat me not to leave thee, but convert me to
    the truth";
So spake in sorrow and in tears the gently chiding
    Ruth.
"Entreat me not to leave thee, nor unclasp thy
    loosening hand;
I'll follow thee, my mother, to the far Judæan land."
But, turning still in grief away from her young,
    pleading face,
And sadly putting back the arms so fondly that
    embrace,

A STORY OF DAUGHTER-LOVE

"My daughter," thus Naomi said in measured tones
 and deep,
"We have our Sabbaths in that land, and holy days
 to keep;
 And there's a bound we cannot pass upon that
 day, you know."
 But Ruth said, "Only where thou goest, mother,
 will I go."

 Still spake Naomi, "Turn again; thy home is not
 with me;
 For Judah's children must not with the outcast
 Gentile be."
 Ruth answered, "In that stranger land with thee,
 O let me stay,
 And where thou lodgest I will lodge; I cannot
 go away."
 And then again Naomi, "We have precepts to
 observe,
 And from our fathers' worship are commanded not
 to swerve."
 Ruth answered with religious zeal, "I bow to
 Judah's Lord:
 Thy people shall my people be; thy God shall be
 my God."

—*Selected.*

HOW A BOY GREW IN GRACE

(*As Samuel might have told the story*)

I WAS an answer to prayer. Mother often used to tell me how sorrowful she was before I was born, because she had no children, and how she went to God's house, and prayed earnestly that she might have "a man child," and she promised God that, if He would send her a little son of her own, she would give him unto the Lord all the days of his life.

God heard her prayer, and answered it, as He has often heard and answered your prayers and mine; and I was that little man child that she asked for. I suppose she always thought of me as God's answer to her prayer. She often told me the story; and, whenever she spoke my name, she said it with so pleasant, happy a voice that it always made me remember that I was "asked of God." Perhaps you were asked of God too. She told me of the promise she had made to God, and as soon as I was old enough to be away from her she took me to God's house at Shiloh. Eli, the aged priest who ministered there, seemed surprised to see us; and my mother said to him: "I am the woman that stood by thee here, praying unto the Lord. For this child I prayed, and the Lord hath given me my petition which I asked of him; therefore also I have lent him to the Lord; as long as he liveth he shall be lent to the Lord."

I was pretty lonesome when my mother said good-by, and went away, leaving me with Eli; but I was glad to remember that I was lent to the Lord, and I believe God was pleased, just as He would be pleased to-day with any boy who would lend himself to the Lord to work for Him all the days of his life.

Every day I "ministered before the Lord," doing little errands for Eli, lighting the lamps, and opening the doors of the house of the Lord every morning, and watching for every little thing I could do to help, because I knew that I was lent to the Lord, and I wanted to please Him every day.

Once every year my mother came up to Shiloh to see me, and every time she brought a little coat that she had made for me. I wonder if you can understand how I loved those little coats, just because my mother made them, though I wore every day when I was ministering in God's house a little linen garment very much like the one Eli wore.

Every year I grew a little stronger, and a little

taller, and a little wiser; and always I felt that the Lord was with me. Once there came a time when God Himself gave me a message for Eli. It was when I was all alone in the night that God called me. I thought it was Eli, and I ran to him quickly and asked what he wanted; and, though at first he thought I had just been dreaming, yet afterward, when I had heard the voice three times, he knew that God was calling to me, and so he told me that, if the voice came again, I must answer, "Speak, Lord, for thy servant heareth;" and I did as he said, and God gave me the message.

It was a very sad message, and I hated to tell it to Eli, for God had said that He would send him great sorrow, and that it was because Eli's own sons had been very wicked, and he had not "restrained them." I never knew before that God sometimes punishes parents because they have not trained their children to do right. I suppose Eli had often wished that they would not do so many wrong and wicked things, but he had not "restrained them"; and so he was punished as well as they.

Very soon after this it came to pass that there was war with the Philistines, and both of Eli's sons were killed in battle, and the ark of God was carried away into the enemy's country, and Eli himself died from the great shock of all this bad news coming at once.

But, though Eli was dead, all the days of my life I ministered before the Lord, and always I felt that the Lord was with me; and as I grew tall and strong in body, and strong in mind, I tried to grow strong in soul too. I think God wants us all to grow strong in those three ways, and as one of Christ's disciples afterward wrote, we must "grow in grace and in the knowledge of our Lord Jesus Christ."

THE GIANT-KILLER

(As David might perhaps have told the story)

I WAS only a shepherd boy, taking care of my father's sheep on the Bethlehem hillside. I was the youngest of seven brothers. One day, while I was tending my sheep, a servant came hurrying to me, saying that the prophet Samuel had come to Bethlehem, and my father wanted me to come at once; so I left my sheep with the servant, and hurried home.

I found all the family waiting for me; and as soon as Samuel saw me he said, "This is the one the Lord hath chosen." Then he anointed me with oil, and told me that sometime I should be king of Israel, but not yet. Then the prophet went away, and I went back to my work; but I had many things to think about now while I was watching my sheep. I thought of King Saul, and of all it meant to be a king; and I thought of the prophet and all that he had said; and then I thought of God, and what kind of man He would want a king to be; and I tried to be such a young man, even now while I was only a shepherd boy.

I used to sing a good deal as I sat there alone on the hillside. I thought of my sheep, and how I took care of them, and fed them, and watered them, and kept them safe from their enemies; and then I thought that just in that same way the Lord took care of me, and I sang a shepherd song. "God is my shepherd," I said to myself; "and while He takes care of me I shall never be in want"; and so, as I thought of all His care for me every day, I wrote the song beginning,

> "The Lord is my shepherd;
> I shall not want."

Since that time many people have sung the same song, and I hope it has helped them as it helped me. Those were happy days when I kept my sheep and sang my songs, and I always trusted God to take care of me as I took care of my sheep.

Once I had a great adventure. Very suddenly one night there came a lion and a bear out of the woods, and carried off one of my lambs. Quickly I went after them, praying all the time in my heart that God would help me. And God heard my prayer, and He did help me, and I killed both the lion and the bear, and saved my lamb. After that I always trusted God, and always when I was in danger I remembered how God had saved me from the lion and the bear, and I knew He could save me again.

There came a time not long after that when the memory of that lion and bear was a great help and comfort to me. My people were fighting against our enemies, the Philistines. My big brothers were in the army, and my father sent me to carry them some food, and to find out how they were prospering. The very day I came to them a great giant came out into the field before all our people, and challenged our army to send out a man to fight him. "Choose you a man to fight with me," he said, "and let him come down to me; if he be able to fight with me, and to kill me, then will we be your servants; but, if I prevail against him and kill him, then you shall be our servants, and shall serve us." And then he said, "I defy the armies of Israel this day; give me a man that we may fight together."

Every day the giant came out and defied our army, and because he was so big a giant no one dared to fight him. When I saw that they were all afraid of him, I said I would go out and fight him. Of course they laughed at me, and asked if I wanted to be killed; but I insisted that the God I trusted would be with me, and would help me to kill the giant; and I was not afraid.

At last they took me to King Saul, and told him that I had offered to fight the giant. The king said that it was impossible that I could kill that great giant, but I told him about the lion and the bear that came out against me, and how God helped me to kill them and get back my lamb, and I said that because God had helped me then I would trust Him to help me now, and with God's help I need not be afraid.

When I went out to meet him, the giant scoffed at me; but I told him I came in the name of my God, and that I believed the God in whom I trusted would help me. Then just with my shepherd's sling I threw a stone, and hit him in the forehead, and killed him; and all the soldiers in his army were afraid and ran, and our soldiers chased them and conquered them.

Many times in my after-life I was in trouble and danger; but I trusted God, and He helped me, and I could always say, "What time I am afraid I will trust in the Lord." Then I learned to say even more than that, for I said, "I will trust in the Lord and *not be afraid.*" Every one who can say that from his heart will find that God will always help him in every trouble.

A SONG OF THE STARRY HEAVENS

(*A Word Picture*)

A LONG, long time ago, in a country far away from here a young shepherd was sitting on a hillside watching his sheep. Day after day he tended them, leading them into green pastures and beside still waters, where they might drink, and protecting them from wild beasts by day and by night.

If I close my eyes, I can almost see him, sitting on a hillside on some still, clear evening, in the moonlight and the starlight, looking up into the starry heavens, and thinking of their wonders and the God who made the stars and the moon. Sitting there in the starlight alone with his sheep, he had much time for thought; and, as he thought, he prayed, "When I consider thy heavens, O Lord, the moon and the stars which thou hast ordained"; and then perhaps he stopped and again "considered the heavens." As he looked and wondered, and "considered," a great thought came to him; and perhaps he sang the words aloud,

"When I consider thy heavens,
The work of thy fingers,
The moon and the stars,

> Which thou hast ordained,
> What is man,
> That thou art mindful of him,
> And the son of man,
> That thou visitest him?"

Then, as he still considered the heavens, and thought of himself just one man alone on the hillside, and other men asleep in their beds, and all so small as compared with all those starry worlds, over and over the thought would come to him, "What is man, that thou art mindful of him?"

Perhaps this would be all he thought the first night; and then, as he sat there night after night considering the heavens, thinking of all the wonders of the starry world and of man's littleness, the thought would come to him that God had given man glory and honor, and set him above all His earthly creatures, and again he would break out into song. "What is man, that thou art mindful of him?" he would sing; "and yet"

> "Thou hast made him a little lower than the angels;
> Thou hast crowned him with glory and honor;
> Thou hast given him dominion over the works of thy hands;
> Thou hast put all things under his feet;
> All sheep and oxen, and the beasts of the field,
> The birds of the heavens and the fish of the sea;
> Whatsoever passeth through the paths of the seas."

And then in closing he would give glory to God who made man and made the starry heavens, as he sings,

> "O Lord, our Lord,
> How excellent is thy name
> In all the earth!"

WHAT THE HEAVENS ARE TELLING

(*A Shepherd's Song*)

DAVID the shepherd boy, the "sweet psalmist of Israel," sat on a hillside watching his sheep and often looking up to the sky, gazing at the stars by night and at the sun by day, and thinking about God, who made heaven and earth, who "counteth the number of the stars," and "calleth them all by their names."

As he sat there day after day and night after night, it seemed to him that the heavens were telling him a story about God who made "the sun to rule by day," and "the moon and stars to rule by night."

"The heavens are telling the glory of God,"

he sang; for only a singer would have had such picture thoughts of the sky; then, as he sang those words, another thought came to him, and again he sang,

"The sky is showing God's handiwork."

I think perhaps he sang those words over and

over; and then, as he sat there with his sheep day after day, a new thought came to him; it seemed as though the days were talking together, one day telling to another stories about God and His wonderful works; and once more he sang, "Day talks unto day, and the nights tell one another wonderful things about God." Perhaps the next evening as he watched his flocks he put his song into words something like those that we read in our Bible today, and sang,

"The heavens are telling the glory of God,
And the sky is showing us His handiwork;
Day is speaking unto day,
And night unto night is showing forth knowledge.

He listened, but he could hear no words; and yet he felt that his song was true, and once more he sang,

"There is no speech nor language;
Their voice is not heard;
Yet their line is gone out
Through all the earth,
And their words to the end of the world."

Perhaps it was in the early morning while he was watching for the sunrise that the next thought came to him; he seemed to have a picture in his mind of the sun having his home in a tent among the stars, and coming every morning out of his door in the sky, and rejoicing as a strong man to run a race, way across the heavens from one end to the other, and then at night going back to his tent among the stars, only to start out the next day and run his race again; and once more he sang,

> "In them hath he set a tent for the sun,
> Which is as a bridegroom
> Coming out of his chamber,
> Rejoicing as a strong man to run a race.
> His going forth is from
> The end of the heavens,
> And his circuit unto the ends of it;
> There is nothing hid from the heat thereof."

Many other thoughts came to that lonely man on the hillside, and he put them all into his song, which we call the nineteenth Psalm, thoughts about God's law, and the blessings that come from obedience to it, and prayers for help to obey it; and then he closes his song with the prayer, which is good for all of us to pray,

> "Let the words of my mouth
> And the meditation of my heart,
> Be acceptable in thy sight,
> O Lord, my strength and my redeemer."

DAVID'S STORY ABOUT HIS SON ABSALOM

(*Father-Love*)

Of all my sons I think I loved Absalom the best, though I am afraid I did not always show my love in the wisest manner. He was so tall, so handsome, so brave! How could I help loving him?

He had grieved me in many ways before he stole away my kingdom; but I think the more he grieved me, the more I loved him, and longed to bring him back into right ways. But he seemed to think only of himself and his own wishes.

There came a time when he wanted the kingdom for himself, and he had no thought for the father who loved him so. He so wanted to be a king himself that he deliberately set himself to win away the hearts of my people from their rightful king. It was easy to make them love him, for he made himself very friendly with every one. Often he said to them, "If I were king, such things as you complain of should not be allowed in the kingdom. I would see that every wrong was righted; I would be a real friend to all my people"; and, as he talked in his pleasant way, it was easy for them to believe him.

When he thought the right time had come, he tried to cover his wickedness with a cloak of goodness. He asked that he might go up to Hebron to pay a vow that he had made unto God; but I think he forgot all about the vow when he reached Hebron, for I never heard of his fulfilling it. He had himself proclaimed king, and many people cheered for him, and I had to hurry away from Jerusalem; but I loved him still, for I was his father.

When my soldiers went out to battle against him, I charged them over and over again, "Deal gently, for my sake, with the young man, even with Absalom." But, alas! I never saw my dear son again. When the messengers came hurrying back to tell me of the victory, my first question was, "Is the young man Absalom safe?" Sorrowfully they told me that he was dead, for they knew how I loved him; and I went up alone into the little chamber over the gate to mourn for my dear son, for he was very dear to me though he had been so wicked.

Then the victory was turned into mourning, for I could not rejoice with my people when my dear son had been killed; and the people walked about sorrowfully as if there had been defeat instead of victory, for I only covered my face, and mourned, "O my son Absalom, my son, my son Absalom! would God I had died for thee, O Absalom, my son, my son!"

I kept on with my mourning and wailing for my son until General Joab had to remind me that I was a king as well as a father, and with a sorrowful heart I went back to my kingdom and my people.

I have often wondered whether Absalom ever knew how much I loved him. To the very last I would have forgiven him and helped him if he would have let me. I wonder whether other boys know how their fathers love them and want to help them. A father's love is too deep and strong and true to be lightly forgotten or thrown away. Always believe that your father loves you, however he shows it or forgets to show it; and try to show him that you love him too. Believe always the words that Solomon wrote, for they are very true,

"A wise son maketh a glad father."

THE BIBLE THAT WAS LOST AND FOUND AGAIN

(A story of promises made to God)

IF you and I had lived hundreds of years ago, in the days of King Josiah, in the land that we now call the Holy Land, we might have gone to a wonderful meeting, and we might have heard some wonderful words read from a book which every one seemed to think was very precious.

We should have gone to the temple, where all the people worshipped, and we should have seen the king himself standing by one of the pillars of the temple, while a very great multitude of people stood around listening. Perhaps we should have asked softly, from some man who stood near, why all these people had gathered, and what was the book to which they were all so eager to listen. And I am sure we should have looked with wonder at the great company of priests and prophets, of royal people and common people; and we should have been very eager to know what had happened to bring together so great a company.

And then I think that some one who stood near

would have told us that a book had been found in the temple, a book that had been lost for many years, and that this was God's book, and God's laws were written in it; and it also told of the rewards that God had promised to those who kept His laws, and of punishments for those who disobeyed them. I think that this man who stood near us would have said that he wanted very much to hear God's laws and obey them, and perhaps he would have asked us to be very quiet that we might hear them read.

And then I think we should have listened eagerly, for I hope that we too should have wanted to know God's laws and obey them. As we listened, we might perhaps have heard a priest, or one of the prophets, read in a loud voice, very distinctly, some of the words that we can read for ourselves to-day in the book of Deuteronomy, closing, it may be, with some such words as these:

"Ye stand this day all of you before the Lord your God. See, I have set before thee life and good, and death and evil, in that I command thee this day to love the Lord thy God, to walk in his ways, and to keep his commandments. Keep, therefore, the words of this covenant, and do them, that ye may prosper in all that ye do."

And then, when the reading was ended, we

should have seen the king in his royal robes, and all the nobles, and the priests, and the common people, promise before the Lord, that "with all their heart and soul they would perform the words of this covenant that are written in this book"; and I hope we should have joined with them in that promise; and that would have meant just what we promise in our Christian Endeavor pledge. May the Lord help us all to keep our promises!

STORY OF A COVETOUS MAN

"Thou Shalt Not Covet"

(*As Gehazi might tell it*)

I WAS the servant of a prophet. I lived with him day by day, and watched his daily life; and I noticed that he never seemed to think of himself, but only of others whom he might help.

Now it happened, through the word of the Lord, that a great man came to my master's home. He was a Syrian captain, who had some time before, among other Hebrew prisoners of war, brought home a little maiden who waited upon his wife. She was a faithful little maid, and, being sorry for the great captain who was suffering from the awful disease of leprosy, had said one day to her mistress, "Would God my lord were with the prophet that is in Samaria; for he would recover him of his leprosy." And so through this kindly thought of hers the great Syrian captain had come to my master to be cured of his leprosy.

When he came with his chariots and horsemen in great splendor, I was filled with envy; and I wished I could have some of his money and his

STORY OF A COVETOUS MAN 75

power. My master did not even trouble to go out and speak to him, but sent a messenger to tell him to go and wash seven times in the Jordan and he would be healed; for Elisha was sure that, if in this way he would show his faith in God, then God would heal him.

Captain Naaman was at first quite indignant, and asked why he could not just as well bathe in one of the rivers in his own country; but his servants persuaded him to do just what Elisha had said, and it was not long before he came back from the Jordan a very different man, for he was now strong and well without a trace of leprosy.

The great captain was very grateful; and he had come back, not only to say, "Thank you," but also to say that through this wonderful miracle he had come to believe in Elisha's God. "Behold, now I know," he said, "that there is no God in all the earth but in Israel; now, therefore, I pray thee, take a blessing of thy servant."

I began to wonder what kind of a present he would give, and to wish he would give me something too. But Elisha said, "As the Lord liveth, before whom I stand, I will receive nothing."

The captain earnestly urged him to take a present of some kind, but Elisha would not. He had not healed him for money. So Captain Naaman went away with his chariot and his horses and all his soldiers, and gave my master nothing. I was much displeased, for I coveted his money. I knew the commandments, and I knew that one of them was, "Thou shalt not covet"; but I did not stop to think of that. I was like many people who live to-day. I wanted something that was not mine, and I wanted it so much that I was willing to do anything to get it. My first sin was coveting what was my neighbor's, and my second was lying. I ran after Captain Naaman as fast as I could; and, when he saw me coming, he stopped, and asked what I wanted. Without stopping a moment to think I said, "My master has sent me, because two young men, sons of the prophets, have just come; and he would be glad if you would give them a talent of silver and two changes of garments." He was very generous, and insisted on my taking two talents of silver, and the garments, and sent two of his servants back with me to carry the gifts.

That did not suit me very well, for I was afraid Elisha would see them; so, when we were nearly back, I told them they need not trouble to go the rest of the way; I would carry the gifts myself. So they gave them to me and went away; and I hid them in a safe place, and then went in to wait upon my master as usual.

STORY OF A COVETOUS MAN 77

I was much disturbed when my master said, "Where have you been, Gehazi?" I thought I just had to tell another lie then to cover up the first one; so I said, "I have not been anywhere." My first sin of coveting had led now to two other sins, for I had told two lies, and had also done something that was very much like stealing in keeping for myself what Captain Naaman thought he was giving to Elisha.

My sin was great, and my punishment had already begun; for I now had no pleasure in the things I had coveted and lied for. But I had to endure another punishment, for Elisha said, "Did not my heart go with you when the man turned again from his chariot to meet you? Is this a time to receive money and gifts?" Then he said that I should have to bear the leprosy that had been Naaman's, and I went out from his presence a leper.

I know now that, even if I had not had such an awful punishment, I should never have enjoyed the things I had coveted; for my conscience troubled me from the moment I took the gifts, and I wished them back. I do not wonder now that afterward Jesus Himself said to a man who coveted riches, "Take heed, and beware of covetousness; for a man's life consisteth not in the abundance of the things which he possesseth." I know that is true now, and I know that the man who breaks the tenth commandment is not nearly so happy as the man who does not covet, but has learned that the Bible is right in saying,

"Let your conversation be without covetousness, and be content with such things as ye have."

A STORY OF ANGEL CHARIOTS

(*A Lesson in Trust, A Word Picture*)

IF you and I had lived away back in the days of "once upon a time," in the land of Israel, we might have made a visit to the prophet Elisha in the little hill town called Dothan; and there I think we should have learned a lesson in trust that we could never forget.

Perhaps we should have heard the young man who was Elisha's servant getting up very early one morning to go up on the hilltop, and we might have followed him. If we had seen him looking off anxiously over the plain, I think we should have looked with him, and then we should have seen what he saw. There was a beautiful view to be seen from that hilltop in northern Syria; but he was not looking at the view, for there, just below us, we should have seen a great company of soldiers and horsemen and chariots, surrounding the hill on all sides, so that no one could get away from the city. No wonder he looked anxious and troubled, and I think we should have been troubled too as we asked him why they were there.

I suppose he would have told us then that all that great army had come out against one man; for they were all afraid of the prophet Elisha, and those Syrian generals and soldiers felt that they could never conquer the Israelites so long as Elisha, the man of God, was there to help them and advise them.

As we saw the young man looking so anxious, I think you and I should have felt more and more afraid, and we should have asked him whether there were soldiers enough in the little city to defend it, and perhaps his answer would have been something like this: " O, no, there is only a handful of soldiers here; and, even if there were many more, my master would not call them out; he just trusts in God to take care of him, and he always feels sure that God will do just what is best for him; so he never seems to be afraid of anything. No, there is nothing we can do; they will surely kill my master, and probably all the rest of us too." And then I think you and I might have been so frightened that we should have wished we had not come to Dothan, and we should have hurried with the young man to Elisha, and should have listened anxiously for Elisha's answer as the young man asked, "Alas! my master, what shall we do?"

A STORY OF ANGEL CHARIOTS 81

And then, as we looked at Elisha, with his white hair and his calm, trustful face, I think we should have grown trustful too, even though we did not see how help could come to us. How surprised we should have been when he answered, "Don't be afraid; for they that are with us are more than they that are with them." What could he mean? How could there be more with us in this defenceless little city than there were with those generals down below?

And then what do you think Elisha did? Why he just lifted up his eyes to heaven, and spoke to God, as if God were right there. "Lord, I pray thee, open his eyes that he may see," he said; and I think we should all have felt that the Lord was with us there, and that we could trust Him to take care of us. And then, if the Lord had opened our eyes as well as those of the young man, we should have seen just what he saw; for "the Lord opened the eyes of the young man, and he saw; and, behold, the mountain was full of horses and chariots of fire round about Elisha."

And so we should have learned the same lesson of trust that the young man learned, as we looked at the angel guards and the fiery chariots all round about Elisha; and I hope we should have learned to feel as Elisha did, that God can always take care of us, whether by angel guards or in some other way. We cannot see the angel guards round about us; but I think perhaps there may be angels around us all the time, watching us and guarding us. Let us try, then, always to "trust and obey"; and let us always mean those words when we sing them.

A BRAVE QUEEN

(As Esther might have told the story)

WE were all very much interested when we heard that the king had ordered that all the fair young maidens in all the provinces should be gathered together and brought to Shushan the palace, and that the maiden who should please the king would be crowned as queen. In every home people were talking of the royal proclamation, and wondering who would be the queen.

I was surprised when my cousin Mordecai brought me to Shushan, and much more surprised when after a time I was told that the king had chosen me to be his queen. I was only a Jewish maiden, and had never dreamed that such an honor would come to me. My cousin Mordecai, who had taken care of me ever since I was a little child, advised me not to say to any one that I was a Jewess; and, because I loved him and knew that he was wiser than I, I obeyed him in the palace, as I had obeyed him at home. It was a great comfort to me in the palace to know that I had a faithful friend outside, whom I could always trust.

One day my servants told me sad news about Mordecai. They said that he had put on sackcloth and ashes, which was always a sign of mourning, and that he had gone out into the midst of the city, crying with a loud and bitter cry. He had come, they said, even before the king's gate, though no one might enter into the king's gate clothed with sackcloth. They told me, too, that many of the Jews were fasting and weeping and wailing, and many lay in sackcloth and ashes. I was very much grieved when I heard this, and I sent other clothing to Mordecai, and told my servants to ask him to take off the sackcloth; but he would not receive the clothing I sent.

Then I sent Hatach, one of the king's chamberlains, who had been appointed to attend on me, and asked him to find out what the trouble was. Then Mordecai sent me word that the wicked Haman had persuaded the king to make a decree that all the Jews in the whole land should be put to death. Mordecai said that it was my duty to go to the king and plead for my people. I was very much frightened when I heard this message, and I sent Hatach back to say to Mordecai, "All the king's servants, and the people of the king's provinces, do know, that whosoever, whether man or woman, shall come unto the king into the inner court, who is not called, there is one law of his to put him to death, except such to whom the king shall hold out the golden sceptre, that he may live; but I have not been called to come in unto the king these thirty days."

I hoped that, when Mordecai knew that I might be killed if I should go in to see the king without being called, he would send me word that I had better not go; but, when his answer came, it was something like this: "You need not think that you will escape any more than all the Jews, even though you are the queen. If you will not try to save your people, we may possibly find help in some other way; but I truly think that God has brought you to the kingdom for such a time as this." Then I sent this message to Mordecai: "Please ask all the Jews to pray for me, and I and my maidens will pray; and after three days I will go to the king and ask him to save my people; and, if I must die, then I will die."

For three days I prayed for courage to do what was right, and then, though I was very much afraid, I put on my very prettiest dress, and went to the king's palace. As I stood there before the king, frightened and trembling, wondering whether he would hold out the golden sceptre to me or would order me to be killed, he smiled, and held out his sceptre. Then I invited the king and the wicked Haman to a banquet; and, while they were there together, I told the king how Haman had plotted against my people. The king was very angry with Haman, and ordered him put to death; and my people were saved.

So my life was spared, after all, and my people were saved; and the Jews had a great day of gladness and feasting, and they decreed that the "days of Purim," as they called them, should always be kept, that every year, in every Jewish family in every land, they should celebrate two days, "as the days wherein the Jews rested from their enemies, and the month which was turned unto them from sorrow to joy, and from mourning into a good day; that they should make them days of feasting and joy, and of sending portions one to another, and gifts to the poor."

To this day the Jews in every land celebrate the feast of Purim in memory of that happy day. I am so glad to be remembered as the queen who saved her people. But what if I had failed because I was afraid? I am glad I could say what you can always say when you are afraid,

"In God have I put my trust;
I will not be afraid what man can do unto me."

A STORY ABOUT LENDING UNTO THE LORD

(As Job might have told it)

I WAS a rich man who lived in the land of Uz. I had ten children who were the joy of my heart, and I had great possessions, including thousands of sheep and camels and oxen, and many servants. Although there were many around me who worshipped idols, yet I was one that feared God, and turned away from evil, and tried to do what was right in God's sight. Every day I offered sacrifices to God, and prayed for my children, and asked God's forgiveness for any sins they might have committed.

We were all very prosperous and happy, but there came a time when God saw fit to try me. In one day all my children were killed in a sad accident; a band of enemy soldiers came up against my servants, and carried away my oxen and asses; my sheep were struck by lightning and many of them killed; and the Chaldeans carried away my camels, and killed the servants who had been guarding them.

All this was a great sorrow to me; and yet that was not all; soon I had another trouble to bear, for I was attacked by a very painful disease, and had to endure great suffering.

Then some of my friends came to comfort me, and they said that it was because of my sins that all this trouble had been sent upon me. They said that, though people had thought I was good, I must really have been living a wicked life in secret, and God was punishing me; but I knew they were wrong in that, for I had honestly tried to live a life that was pleasing to God. I told them of the life I had lived before them in the land of Uz, and how people had honored me and loved me. "When the ear heard me," I said, "then it blessed me; and when the eye saw me, it gave witness to me, because I delivered the poor that cried, and the fatherless, and him that had none to help him. I was eyes to the blind, and feet was I to the lame. I was a father to the poor, and the blessing of him that was ready to perish came upon me."

I did not mean to boast about my kindness to the poor; but I told them these things that they might know that I was really trying to live such a life as God would approve, and that my troubles could not have been sent as a punishment for sin. I learned many things about God that I might never have learned except for my troubles; and at last I was able to say unto the Lord, "I have heard of thee by the hearing of the ear, but now mine eye seeth thee."

I was always glad for everything I had done to help the poor and suffering, and in the end I learned how true it is that "he that hath pity upon the poor lendeth unto the Lord; and that which he hath given will he pay him again." The Lord did repay me; He gave me children, and friends, and much happiness in the later years of my life; and I can say as the wise man said long after, "He that hath mercy on the poor, happy is he."

A STORY OF A MAN WHO TRIED TO RUN AWAY FROM GOD

(As Jonah might tell the story)

God's call came to me very plainly, and I knew He wanted me to go to Nineveh, and warn the people that their city was to be destroyed; but I did not want to go. It may have been partly because I was a coward, for I knew how great and wicked a city it was; and the people might be very angry, and perhaps try to kill me. But I am afraid it was partly because I felt that God's warning was meant to lead them to repentance, that He might pardon them; and I did not really want them to be forgiven, for, like all the Jews, I hated the Ninevites. And so I shirked my duty, and tried to run away from God.

I don't suppose I really thought that I could hide away from God, but I just wanted to get as far away from Nineveh as I could; and then perhaps I should forget God's call to me, and could put those wicked people out of my mind.

But God does not want us to put the wicked out of our mind. He wants us to show them the way

TRIED TO RUN AWAY FROM GOD 91

back to God, and He is calling every one to-day just as truly as He called me, to do all that we can to help people who have wandered away from Him to find the way back, whether they are in heathen lands or in our own land.

I went down to Joppa, and, finding a ship going to Tarshish, I paid my fare, and went on board; but I did not get away from my conscience or from God. I was so worn out with fighting against God that I went down below, and soon fell asleep; I had found, as many others have found, that it is harder to fight against one's plain duty than to do it. I did not sleep long, though; for a great storm came up, and I was awakened by the frightened sailors, who did not know what to do. They had prayed to their own gods, but found no comfort or help there. They had cast out much of their cargo into the sea to lighten the ship, but it did no good. What should they do next? They had concluded that, if I would pray to my God, He might perhaps be more powerful, or more willing to help them; and so they came to me, saying, "Arise; call upon thy God, if so be that God will think upon us that we perish not." They did not know that God is thinking of us all the time, and is always waiting for us to call upon Him.

They asked me many questions, too, for they

thought that it must be for my sake that this storm had come upon them. Then I said to them plainly, "I am a Hebrew, and I fear the Lord, the God of heaven, which hath made the sea and the dry land." I confessed to them that I had been trying to run away from my duty, and advised them to throw me into the sea, as I believed that if they did that God would save their lives. Very reluctantly they did as I said, but not until they too had prayed to my God, the true God who made heaven and earth. And so, though I had been unwilling to be a missionary to the people of Nineveh, I had become a willing missionary to those heathen sailors, and they had learned something of the true God and His power.

Then they threw me down into the sea, and the Lord had prepared a great fish to swallow me up; for three days God kept me alive inside the fish, and then I was once more cast forth, but this time on the dry land.

If you want to know how I felt when I was sinking way down into the depths of the sea, and the floods compassed me about, and the seaweeds were wrapped about my head, then you must read the prayer that I prayed and afterward wrote down that you might read it. I was like many people who are alive now; when I was in trouble, I prayed unto the Lord. I think perhaps that is one great reason why God allows trouble to come upon us, because it drives us to Him. If we always lived a life of prayer, I do not believe we should have so many troubles; and we should certainly have more grace to bear the troubles that must come.

And so I learned the lesson that every one must learn in some way, that we cannot get away from the presence of God, that He is always looking down upon us; that "his eyes behold, his eyelids try, the children of men." I learned, too, that it is always harder to shirk our duty than it is to do it. The only right way for any of us is to ask God every day what He would have us do, and then do it. And so my last message to you to-day is,

"Whatsoever he saith unto you, do it."

THE STORY OF THE FIRST CHRISTMAS

(As one of the shepherds might have told it)

WE were just a little company of shepherds, tending our sheep in the fields outside the little town of Bethlehem. It was a cold night, and we had kindled a little fire of sticks, that we might warm ourselves once in a while; we sat around the fire in the starlight talking together, while two or three of the men, tired with the day's work, had fallen asleep. It happened that much of our talk that night had been about the Coming One, of whom we had often heard the rabbis speak. They said He would be born in Bethlehem, and some thought it would be soon, while others felt sure that it would not be in our time.

I wondered how He would come, and what He would be like, and what He would do for the world. Some thought He would come in splendor as a great king, and would rule righteously over our people Israel, and that we should no longer be oppressed by cruel rulers and Roman tax-gatherers; but I was doubtful. It did not seem to me that the promises and prophecies which I had heard the rabbis read in our synagogues meant just that, and I had given much thought to it as I watched my flocks by night. Of one thing I felt sure; I knew that I should love Him and serve Him; and O, how I hoped He would come in my time!

At last we grew drowsy, and the rest of the men fell asleep, while I sat quietly by the fire, thinking of all we had talked of. Suddenly, as I sat there in the firelight and the starlight, a wonderful light shone round about me, more wonderful and glorious than anything I had ever seen. I roused the sleeping shepherds, and we all saw the light, and were afraid. What was it, and what did it mean?

While we wondered and trembled, suddenly we saw a beautiful angel standing in the midst of the wonderful light; and he called to us in a loud, clear voice. "Fear not," he said; "I bring you good tidings of great joy, which shall be to all people." And then He told us that the little child Christ had already come, and we should find the little baby lying in a manger in a stable in Bethlehem. Then, as suddenly as the angel himself had come, there came a whole choir of angels, singing the most wonderful song ever heard on earth.

"Glory to God in the highest;
And on earth peace, good will toward men,"

they sang; and then, all in a moment, the angels were gone, and we were left alone.

For a few moments we stood there quietly, waiting to see whether the angels would come again; but all was peaceful, beautiful starlight as before. Then I started up, and said, "Come, let us go to Bethlehem, and see the thing which has come to pass, which the Lord has made known to us."

You may be sure that we hurried as fast as our feet could carry us, and we found Mary and Joseph, and the blessed Christ-child lying in a manger, just as the angel had said; and we bowed down and worshipped the Child.

After telling our story of the angels, and talking with Joseph and Mary, we went back to our sheep, but slowly and thoughtfully, stopping to tell the wonderful "good tidings of great joy" to every one we met, for it was early morning by this time. We were all "glorifying and praising God" all the way back, for all that we had heard and seen that holy night. We could never forget that first Christmas, as we call the blessed Christ-child's birthday now, and we always remembered the angels' song and message; all our lives after that we tried, so far as we could, to carry joy to all people, and to help make peace on earth, good will to men. That is what the blessed Saviour wants us all to do all our lives, and every time His birthday comes around it should remind us once more of the work He came to do, and the work He wants us to do for Him.

FRIENDS OF CHRIST

(As Andrew might have told the story)

I was one of the very first of Christ's disciples, and I have always been so glad, because I had His friendship so much the longer. I only wish I might have known Him even when He was a boy, for I am sure He was a boy that every one loved.

I was only a common fisherman, living near the Sea of Galilee and going out in my boat every day with my brother Simon; but I had often thought about the Coming One who was to be our Saviour, and had longed to know more about Him, and had wondered whether it could be possible that I should ever see Him.

We had often heard about John the Baptist and about the crowds who went to hear him preach, and how he baptized a great many of them if they were sorry for their sins and wanted to do right. Sometimes we used to go and listen to his preaching, and I called myself one of his disciples.

One day I was standing with John, one of my near neighbors, listening to John the preacher, when all at once he pointed to a young man who was passing by, and said, "Behold the Lamb of God, that taketh away the sin of the world!" As soon as we heard that, John and I followed after Him that we might know where He lived. Presently He turned, and seeing us following Him, said, "What are you seeking?" John said, "Master, where do you live?" "Come and see," He said; and we went with Him. As He talked with us, we felt sure that this was really the Christ. He let us stay with Him all that day, both hearing Him and asking Him questions; and from that time we always counted ourselves among His friends.

As soon as I could I went and found my brother Simon, and I said to him, "We have found the Christ!" And I brought him to Jesus, and he too believed on Him. It was not long before others came to Him, and after a time He chose twelve of His followers, who should be His special friends and be near Him always, and I was so glad that He chose me for one of the twelve! He said He had called us that we might be with Him, and that He might send us forth to do His errands; and often He sent us out to preach and to teach, and others learned to believe on Him through our teaching.

So long as He lived on earth we followed Him, until that very last night, when He was betrayed into the hands of His enemies; and then—I have always felt so sorry and ashamed to remember that we all forsook Him and fled! And to think that I, who was one of His first followers, was one of the first to run away! But He forgave us, and blessed us, and gave us work to do for Him after He was gone; and He promised to be always with us to help us, even though we could not see Him. "Lo, I am with you alway, even unto the end of the world," He said; and many times we felt His presence with us when we could not see Him. That promise is for all those who are His friends to-day just as much as it was for us.

I was never able to do as much for Him as my brother Simon, whom Jesus named Peter; indeed, many of the others did more than I could do, for I was one of the quiet ones, who could not talk as Peter could, but I have always been glad to remember that it was I who brought Peter to Christ, and that, when our Master fed the five thousand, I was the one to suggest that the little lad's loaves and fishes might be used by Christ.

Sometimes, when I have felt that I was not worthy to be called His friend, I have been glad to remember that He once said, "You are my friends, if you do whatsoever I command you;" and I like to think that all those who are trying now to keep His commandments have a right to call themselves His friends.

FOLLOWING CHRIST

(As Matthew might tell the story if he could come back)

I WAS a tax-gatherer, about my regular business in the custom-house when Jesus called me to follow Him. I had heard of the wonderful things He did, and the wonderful words He spoke, and I had longed to see Him. I had heard that He had called some of the fishermen on the lake to be His disciples. Just common, every-day fishermen they were; but I know they must have been earnest, faithful men, or He would not have chosen them. How I wished He would call me! But that, I thought, could never be, for all men despised me because of my business.

One day as I sat at the receipt of custom not far from the Sea of Galilee, taking the tax money from the many travellers who journeyed from Damascus to the seashore with their goods, I saw a small boat come across the lake and land near Capernaum. Soon a great crowd gathered around a stranger who had come in the boat, and I wondered whether it might perhaps be Jesus of Nazareth, for I knew that He now called Capernaum "His own city." But they were too far away for me to see plainly, and I could not leave my business.

A few days later I saw a great crowd coming from Capernaum down "the way of the sea." I asked a man what was going on, and he said, "Jesus of Nazareth is passing by; the crowds follow Him." This was my opportunity to see Him, and I was so glad! He saw me sitting there at my money-table, and to my great surprise and joy He called *me*. You may be sure it did not take me long to put away my money and my table and follow Him. I invited Him to a feast at my house, and He honored me by coming; and, although the Pharisees scoffed, saying, "Why does He eat with publicans and sinners?" I did not care for their scoffs, for He had called *me;* and from that day I followed Him as one of His disciples.

A good many years afterward, when I had read some of Paul's letters to the churches, I said to myself: "Why does not some one write the story of the Master's life? Why should not *I* do it?" I was quite used to writing because of my former business, and why should I not use my pen to write something worth while, that all the world might read the story of Jesus?

I wrote especially for the Jews, that they might know that Jesus was the Messiah who had been promised; and often I quoted for them a prophecy that had been fulfilled. But of all the stories of His life that I wrote I liked best to write of the times when He called us to be disciples, and we left all and followed Him. I like to remember that He called Peter and Andrew and John and James from their fishing, and me from my custom-house, and all of the twelve from their every-day work, just as He calls people now, and O, the difference it made in our lives when we heard Him say, "Follow me," and obeyed His call!

He is calling you to-day, and, though it is only in your hearts that you hear His voice, He is saying to you now, as He said to me, "Follow me." I gave up all my business and everything that might have hindered me, and followed Him. Are you ready to give up everything that has hindered you, and begin to-day to follow Jesus?

HOW JESUS KEPT THE SABBATH

(*As the man with the withered hand might have told it*)

I WAS a man with a withered hand, and there were many things that other people could do that I could not; always it had been a great trouble and hindrance to me, but it could not be cured.

At last, however, there came a time when I began to hear wonderful stories about Jesus of Nazareth; how He always went about doing good, and how He had healed many people with different kinds of illness; and I began to wonder whether He could perhaps make my poor, useless hand strong and well again.

I had heard that, wherever He might be, He always went to the synagogue on the Sabbath day, and the people always crowded there, and listened eagerly as He told them of things as God would have them; and often I wished that sometime I too might see Him and hear Him.

One day I heard that He had come to Capernaum, and on the Sabbath day I hurried to the synagogue, and found Him there teaching the people "the things concerning the kingdom." I crowded to the front, and listened with the rest, eager to hear His words, and hoping that I might be healed. By and by I noticed that some of the Pharisees were looking at Jesus, and others were scowling at me, watching to see whether I would ask to be healed; and I knew they would say that Jesus was breaking the fourth commandment and working on the Sabbath if He healed people on that day.

Jesus did not even wait for me to ask Him, but, calling me by name, He said to me, "Stand forth." At once I went forward, and stood there alone in the midst of the crowd, while the Pharisees angrily watched. Jesus knew what they were thinking, though they had not said anything yet; and His face was sad as He looked upon them and asked sorrowfully, "Is it right to do good on the Sabbath day, or to do evil, to save life, or to kill?" I think they must have felt very much ashamed, for they stood there before Him, answering nothing, while I was just hoping and hoping that He would heal me, whatever they might think or say. Then with a loving, sorrowful look He turned to me, saying, "Stretch forth your hand." At once I believed that I could do it because He said so, though I could not have done it before; and I stretched out my hand, and immediately it was restored, whole and strong as the other one. Oh, how joyful and happy I was, and how I thanked Him! But the Pharisees were not happy, and I heard afterward that they went out and planned how they might kill Him.

Another Sabbath not long afterward I heard that He was teaching in a synagogue not far away, and I hurried there to listen again to His words. There I saw Him heal a poor woman who for eighteen years had not been able to stand up straight; people said of her "she was bowed together, and could in no wise lift herself up." Jesus called her to Him, and laid His hands on her; "and immediately she was made straight, and glorified God."

Again the Pharisees found fault with Him for breaking the Sabbath; and, not daring to say it to Him, they turned to the people, and said, "There are six days in which men ought to work; in them, therefore, come and be healed, and not on the Sabbath day."

Jesus looked at them sadly, and said: "You are living like hypocrites; you are only pretending to be good. Would not each one of you on the Sabbath day untie your ox or your ass, and lead him away to water just because he is thirsty? And ought not this woman, who has been suffering for eighteen years, to be loosed from this bond on the Sabbath day?" When He said this, the Pharisees were ashamed, and could not answer Him; and "all the multitude rejoiced for all the glorious things that were done by him."

And so He taught us that the Sabbath was made for man; that it was meant to be a day for rest and worship, and a day to do good and not evil. We learned, too, that it was His custom to go always on the Sabbath day to the synagogue, and I believe it always pleases Him to find His children in His house on that day; we know, too, that He likes to have us spend the Sabbaths as He did, in doing good and helping others, always remembering that it is the Lord's day.

HOW TO BE GREAT: A LESSON FROM A LITTLE CHILD

(As Peter might have told the story)

WE had been travelling through Galilee, and we came to Capernaum, and went into my home, where I had invited my friends. The Master's face was sad as He looked upon us, and asked, "What were you talking about on the way?"

We looked at one another, and were silent; for with the Master's sad eyes looking into our faces, and into our very hearts, it seemed, we were all so sorry and ashamed that not one of us was willing to tell Him; for on the way we had been quarrelling and disputing over the question which of us was the greatest.

There was Andrew, who had been one of the very first disciples to come to Jesus; and there were James and John, whom He loved to have near Him; and I felt that He had given special tokens of His love for me; and there was Judas, who thought he was really the greatest among us because he was our treasurer; and so for one reason and another almost every one of us had felt that we had some claim to be the greatest, and should have the best place when He should set up His kingdom; for we all expected Him to set up an earthly kingdom when the right time should come. We had had many arguments and much discussion about it on the way; and we had all been more or less angry, and had all had selfish feelings; and now, with Jesus looking at us, we did not want to answer His question; so we all stood there silent and abashed before Him.

He did not need any answer to His question, however, for He knew what was in our hearts just as well as He knows what is in your heart to-day. "If any man would be first," He said quietly, "he shall be last of all and servant of all." Just then one of my little children came running into the room, and Jesus took him up in His arms, and said, "Except you change your lives and become as little children you shall in no wise enter into the kingdom of heaven." And then He added, "Whosoever therefore shall humble himself as this little child, the same is the greatest in the kingdom of heaven." I wish you could have seen the face of that little boy as Jesus held him in His arms and spoke these words; I am sure the boy would never forget, as long as he lived, the loving face of the Master, or the words He spoke that day; and he would always be glad to remember that once Jesus had held him in His arms, and used him to teach a lesson to His disciples.

And so we learned the lesson that it is not those who think themselves great, and seek great things for themselves, who are truly great in God's sight, but those who are humble, and forgetful of themselves, and who try to help others to enter into God's kingdom. As long as I lived I could never look at that little child again without remembering the Master's words; and the story has been written down in God's book so that you may read it, and that you too may remember who are the truly great ones in God's sight.

A BLIND MAN AND HIS NEIGHBORS

(*A Dialogue*)

LOOKING backward across the years, and far away across the seas, to the country which we now call the Holy Land, I seem to see very plainly something that perhaps to-day we should call a moving picture. I seem to see Jesus and His disciples walking along one of the streets of Jerusalem, busily talking as they walk. They meet all kinds of people, but the disciples seem specially interested in a certain blind man, for whom they feel a great pity because they know that he has never seen the beautiful world around him.

"Master," says Peter, "who did sin, this man or his parents, that he was born blind?" Jesus answers, "It is not because this man has sinned or his parents, but that the power of God might be shown in him." A little later Jesus says, "As long as I am in the world I am the light of the world." Then I seem to see Him touching the blind man's eyes as He says, "Go, wash in the pool of Siloam," and the blind man walks away.

Jesus and His disciples go on their way; and, as

A BLIND MAN AND HIS NEIGHBORS

in imagination I linger there, I soon see the blind man coming back, looking around him with wondering, wide-open eyes, upon the beautiful world he has never seen before. A crowd soon gathers around him; and, as I listen, this is what I seem to see and hear:

[*The blind man and three of his neighbors come forward.*]

First Neighbor. Is not this he that sat and begged?

Second Neighbor. It is he.

Third Neighbor. No, but he is like him.

Blind Man. I am he who was blind.

First Neighbor. How were your eyes opened?

Blind Man. The man that is called Jesus made clay, and anointed mine eyes, and said unto me, "Go to Siloam and wash"; so I went away, and washed, and I received sight.

Second Neighbor. Where is he?

Blind Man. I don't know.

Third Neighbor. Let us take him to the Pharisees.

[*They lead him to one side, where three or four Pharisees are standing.*]

First Pharisee. Tell us how you received your sight.

Blind Man. He put clay upon my eyes, and I washed, and do see.

Second Pharisee. This is the Sabbath day!

Third Pharisee. This man is not from God, because he does not keep the Sabbath.

First Pharisee. How can a man that is a sinner do such wonders?

Second Pharisee [*to the blind man*]. What sayest thou of him, that he opened thine eyes?

Blind Man. He is a prophet.

A Jew. Let us ask his parents about it.

Second Jew. I don't believe that the man was really blind.

[*The blind man's father and mother come forward.*]

First Jew. Is this your son, who you say was born blind?

Second Jew. How then does he now see?

The Mother [*to the father in a low tone*]. He must tell them himself. I am afraid they will put us out of the synagogue if we say that the Christ healed him.

The Father [*to the Jews*]. We know that this is our son, and that he was born blind; but how it happens that he can see now we do not know, or who opened his eyes we know not.

A BLIND MAN AND HIS NEIGHBORS

Ask him. He is of age; he shall speak for himself.

First Pharisee [*to the blind man*]. Give glory to God. We know that this man is a sinner.

Blind Man. Whether he is a sinner I know not. One thing I know, that, whereas I was blind, now I see.

Second Pharisee. What did he to thee? How opened he thine eyes?

Blind Man. I told you even now, and you would not hear. Wherefore would you hear it again? Would you also become his disciples?

Third Pharisee. You are his disciple, but we are Moses' disciples. We know that God spoke to Moses, but as for this man we know not whence he is.

Blind Man. Why, herein is a marvel, that you know not whence he is, and yet he opened my eyes. We know that God heareth not sinners; but, if any man be a worshipper of God and do His will, him He heareth. Since the world began it was never heard that any one opened the eyes of a man born blind. If this man were not from God, He could do nothing.

Third Pharisee. Thou wast altogether born in sins, and dost thou teach us?

Second Pharisee. Let us cast him out of the synagogue.

They cast him out of the synagogue, and the crowd slowly scatters, talking still of the wonderful miracle. Some one tells Jesus that the man has been cast out, and at once Jesus goes and finds him, and asks, "Do you believe on the Son of God?" It is no surprise to hear the blind man answer, "Who is He, Lord, that I might believe on Him?" It is very plain from his answer to the Pharisees that he is all ready to believe. I like to think how his face must have lighted up as Jesus said to him, "Thou hast both seen Him, and it is He that talketh with thee." And I like to think of the man's quick answer, "Lord, I believe." And now, as the story ends, I seem to see the man who once was blind kneeling down before his Saviour, and worshipping Him. May his story help us also to believe on the Son of God.

A MAN WHO WAS A GOOD NEIGHBOR

(As a bystander might have told it)

I WAS one of the crowd that was listening to Jesus that day when the lawyer came to him asking, "What shall I do to inherit eternal life?"

"What is written in the law?" asked Jesus. "How readest thou?"

Now the lawyer prided himself on his knowledge of the books of the law, and felt quite able to read and explain all that was written there. I thought he would probably begin to talk about the Ten Commandments, but instead of that he repeated a shorter statement that he had found in Deuteronomy and Leviticus, which really included all the ten. "Thou shalt love the Lord thy God," he said, "with all thy heart, and with all thy soul, and with all thy strength, and with all thy mind; and thy neighbor as thyself."

"Thou hast answered right," said Jesus; "this do and thou shalt live."

The lawyer did not seem to feel troubled about the first commandment, but he was not quite comfortable in his mind about the second one. How about loving his neighbor? How much did this second commandment mean? What did it require of him? "Who is my neighbor?" he asked.

I was rather glad to hear him ask that question, for it did not seem easy to me to love my neighbor as well as I loved myself, and I too wanted to know the answer to this question; so I listened eagerly to see what He would say.

But instead of answering the lawyer's question Jesus told him a story. "A certain man was going down from Jerusalem to Jericho," He said; "and he fell among robbers, who both stripped him, and beat him, and departed, leaving him half dead." We all knew how dangerous that Jericho road was, leading down through narrow, rocky gorges, with many good hiding-places for robbers. Why, I myself had known a man who had been treated in much the same way on this very road; and I wondered whether the man of whom Jesus spoke was perhaps some one He had known.

But Jesus went on with His story. "A certain priest was going down that way," He said; "and, when he saw him, he passed by on the other side." I could easily imagine that priest, hurrying home from a temple service in Jerusalem, too busy with his own affairs, and in too much of a hurry, to stop and help this poor man, who was no relation of his.

A MAN WHO WAS A GOOD NEIGHBOR

I am afraid that we are all like that priest sometimes, too busy with our own affairs to think much about our neighbors, who may be greatly in need of help that we could give. I wondered whether I should have stopped to help the poor man if I had been that priest.

But, while I was thinking about it, Jesus went on with His story. "In like manner a Levite also, when he came to the place, and saw him, passed by on the other side," He said. I could almost see the Levite, humming a tune as he walked along; for I suppose he had been one of the singers at the temple service. I could imagine him saying to himself, as he looked at the poor, wounded man: "I'm sorry for the poor fellow, but I don't see what I can do about it; it isn't really any of my business; I don't know the man. He ought to have known better than to come down this road alone. He will probably die, anyway, and it would not do any good for me to stay here till the robbers come back and attack me too." Then I fancied I could see him crossing over to the other side of the road, and hurrying away as fast as he could.

But, while I was picturing the scene to myself, Jesus went on to tell of a Samaritan man who came along and helped the poor man, binding up his wounds, and carrying him on as far as the inn, and paying the landlord to take care of him until he should be well again. As I listened to the story, I wondered again what I should have done if I had been there. I am afraid we are all of us like the Levite sometimes. We see some one in trouble, and we just content ourselves with saying, "It is too bad! what a pity!" and then we go on our way, and attend to our own affairs, without even trying to help.

Then Jesus turned to the lawyer and said, "Which of these men was neighbor to the one that fell among the robbers?" The lawyer, who had evidently meant to have a long argument, had nothing to say for himself. "The man that helped him was his neighbor," he said.

"Go and do thou likewise," said Jesus. That was all; but we had learned our lesson, and I can never think of that Jericho road without remembering that we have neighbors all around us, who are waiting, perhaps, for us to show ourselves neighborly. I know now that any man who needs my help is my neighbor.

A VISIT FROM JESUS

(*As Martha might have told the story*)

I WAS so glad when I heard that Jesus was coming to Bethany! And, when Lazarus started out to meet Him, I asked him to beg the Master to honor us by coming to our home. Oh, it was such a joy to think of His coming! It seemed to me that I could not do enough for Him. I wanted to do everything I could to honor Him.

I knew how weary He must be, with the crowd always pressing about Him; and He was so kind and loving, and so willing always to give His time and strength to help all those who asked for His help! I wanted to do something for Him that would show Him how much I loved Him; so I planned just the best meal that I could think of, for nothing could be too good for Him. It meant a great deal of work, but I did not care how tired I might get in working for Him. Mary thought I was planning too much; she was afraid we should not have any time to listen to the Master; and she thought perhaps it would please Him better if we should get a simpler meal, and have hearts at leisure to listen to His words. But I thought she was wrong, and went on with my preparations; and, when the Master came, though I gave Him a glad welcome, yet I could hardly stop to speak to Him, lest the dinner should be spoiled.

Mary had helped, and I know now that she did not mean to leave me to do more than my share of the work; but the Master was speaking, and she was eagerly listening, and planning how to live the kind of life He talked of; and I worked on alone; and, though I was working for the Master, my heart was full of bitter thoughts about my sister.

Sometimes the thought came to me that the Master would rather I would leave my busy work, and listen to His teachings; but I put the thought away, and worked on, till I was so tired and cross that I could not stand it any longer; and at last I went to the Master, and said, "Dost Thou not care that my sister did leave me to serve alone?"

What a hard, bitter, mean thing to say! I knew without being told that He would rather have me show a loving spirit than get up the best dinner that was ever cooked. Oh, I was so ashamed when He looked at me so kindly, yet sorrowfully, as if He were looking into my very heart! I knew it was because He saw the love that was there, as well as the bitterness, that His voice was so gentle

A VISIT FROM JESUS 123

and kind, as He told me that I was giving too much importance to little things, and that Mary had chosen the good part which could not be taken away.

I knew He was right, for she would never forget the words she had been listening to, and they would help to make her whole life better. I never forgot His words to me; and, though afterward I had other opportunities to minister to Him, yet I never again let myself be so "cumbered about much serving" as to leave no time to listen to His words. I always tried after that to put first things first, and remembered that the best way to show Him that I loved Him was to listen to Him and obey Him.

A STORY OF LOVING-KINDNESS AND THANKFULNESS

(As it might have been told by one who said, "Thank you")

WE were ten sorrowful men, "standing afar off," and looking wistfully towards a Samaritan village. We were sorrowful, and yet our faces were lighted up with a gleam of hope. We were lepers; but we had heard that Jesus of Nazareth could do wonderful things, and that He cared for all who were sick or sorrowful; and He was coming our way. I was a Samaritan, and the other nine men were Jews; and, if we had all been well, they would have scorned me, for Jews would have nothing to do with Samaritans; but because we all had the same dreadful disease we had become friends in our misery.

Can you think how eagerly we watched as Jesus and His disciples drew near? We stood afar off, for lepers are not allowed to go near other people; and we all called out as loud as we could, "Jesus, Master, have mercy on us." He came towards us with such a loving, pitiful look on His face that I

A STORY OF THANKFULNESS 125

knew He would help us if He could, and some way I felt sure that He could. But what do you think He said? Why, He just said in a quiet voice, "Go show yourselves unto the priests"; and He did not say a word about healing us.

We knew the law required that, if a man were healed of his leprosy, he should go and show himself to the priest; and not until the priest himself declared him healed could he go about among other people. But why did this strange rabbi tell us *now* to go to the priest? We looked at one another doubtfully, and some hesitated; but there was really no question in my mind. The moment He gave the command I felt that I must go, and that I wanted to go, whether He would heal me or not. "Come," I said to the others, "let us do just what He tells us to do"; and without a word we turned and started to go to the priest.

And then a very wonderful thing happened, for as we went we were healed. All at once I felt new life coming to me; and my fingers, which had been decaying with the dreadful disease, became all in a minute whole and sound. My whole body was changed, and I was a well man. We looked at one another with joyful faces, hardly believing our own eyes, as we saw each man looking well and strong. We shouted for joy, and we hurried along as fast as we could in our eagerness to find a priest and be pronounced well and sound. So **happy** were we, and so eager, that for a moment we all forgot the One who had healed us.

But we had taken only a few steps when I suddenly stopped and turned back.

"Where are you going?" asked the others.

"I am going back to thank the Master," I said.

"O, not yet," said the others; "let us see the priest first; we will thank Him some other time."

But my heart was so full that I felt I just must thank Him now; and I went back and fell down at His feet, thanking Him and praising God. And what do you think He said? He looked at me a moment, lovingly yet sadly, and said: "Were there not ten cleansed? But where are the nine? Is this stranger, this Samaritan, the only one who has returned to give glory to God?" and then in a **very** kind and gentle voice, He said, "Arise; go thy way; thy faith hath made thee whole."

I cannot tell you the joy that was in my heart. To think that *He cared* for my poor thanks! And, when He said, "Thy faith hath made thee whole," I felt that not only my body, but my soul, had been healed; and I resolved that all my life I would **try** to live as He would wish me to; for I felt that **my** life belonged to Him, and the best way to **thank**

Him was to try to live such a life as He lived. And so I learned my lesson, that Jesus likes to have us say, "Thank you!" to one another and to God, "who daily loadeth us with benefits." O, I hope you and I will never forget to thank Him by our words and by our lives.

A STORY ABOUT TWO WAYS OF PRAYING

(As it might have been told by a bystander)

JESUS was on His way to Jerusalem. I was one of the crowd that followed Him from place to place, listening to His words, and seeing the miracles He performed. I did not yet believe in Him, but I was curious to hear what this great preacher had to say; and so I followed with the rest, though I was sometimes ashamed of the company in which I found myself; for I was a Pharisee, and considered myself much better than most of the people in the crowd. There were many tax-gatherers among them, and we all despised such people as that, because they were always cheating other people and looking out for themselves first. I knew, too, that some of the people in the crowd were thoroughly bad; and I was always astonished that the Master allowed such men to follow Him.

He had been talking about praying, and I knew that I was all right there, for I prayed very often, and I fasted and gave tithes; and I felt myself to be so much better than most of the people around me that I wanted to hear what He would say to them. But, while I was feeling so well contented

TWO WAYS OF PRAYING 129

with myself, the Master began to tell another story, for much of His teaching began with story-telling. "There were two men," He said, "who went up into the temple to pray, one a Pharisee and one a publican." I knew at once that He would praise the Pharisee for his prayer; for the Pharisees pray often, and pride themselves upon their righteousness. I felt almost sorry for the many publicans in that crowd; for I knew that many of them were wicked men, and of course God would not accept their prayers.

But to my great surprise He began to repeat the words of the prayers that these two men offered. I can seem to see even now the sorrowful look on His face as He repeated the Pharisee's prayer, "God, I thank Thee that I am not as other men, extortioners, unjust, adulterers, or even as this publican. I fast twice in the week; I give tithes of all that I get." I had never prayed in just those words, but I was ashamed to remember that my prayers had often been very much like that. I had not exactly thanked God that I was better than other folks, but I had often had that feeling as I prayed; and I wondered whether the Master had sometimes watched me when I was praying in the temple. O, how ashamed I felt as the Master repeated the Pharisee's words! I counted five times that the Pharisee said "I" in that prayer, and his whole thought seemed to be about himself and how good he was. Why, it was not really a prayer at all; he was just boasting to God about himself and his own goodness, and I knew that my prayers had often been much like that in spirit if not in words.

Then the Master told us of the publican, who, with bowed head, said humbly, "God, be Thou merciful to me, a sinner." That was all he said, just those few words and nothing more; but that was a real prayer. I knew the lesson the Master wanted us to learn, even before He spoke His last words, "This man went down to his house justified rather than the other; for every one that exalteth himself shall be humbled; but he that humbleth himself shall be exalted."

And so I learned my lesson, taught by the Master Himself, that the prayers God loves must be earnest and sincere, and spoken with a humble spirit. I learned then to see myself as God saw me, and I learned how to pray.

Afterward I heard Him speak many other words about prayer; and, as I listened, I felt that, if we would pray aright, we need only remember the Master's words, and pray such prayers as the one He Himself taught His disciples.

JESUS AND THE CHILDREN

(As a mother might have told the story)

I HAD heard many things about Jesus, and I longed to see and hear Him myself. One day I was told that He had come into our neighborhood, and was teaching and preaching and healing the sick.

I was very glad of that, and I said to a neighbor, "The Master has come over Jordan, and the people are crowding around Him. He is teaching and healing the people, sometimes healing them just with a touch of His fingers, they say. And now I shall carry the children, little Rachel, and Samuel and John, and I think I shall even take Baby Esther to Him. If He will only lay His hands on them and bless them, I am sure they will be better children always; for His blessing will follow wherever they go."

But their father heard me, and he said: "What a foolish idea! Why, don't you know how busy the Master is? Do you suppose He would stop to notice the children? Why, you ought not to think of such a thing."

But I said, "O, please don't hinder me; I do so want to go! More than I want anything else in the world I want the Master's blessing for my children."

Then their father said, "All right, you can try it; but I don't believe you can ever get near Him."

My neighbors, too, thought I was foolish. One mother said, "Why, *I* would not do it for anything. I should be afraid the children might get hurt in the crowd." Another said, "I would go with you if I thought it would be any use, but I don't suppose He would want to be bothered with children."

And so they advised against it till even the children began to be afraid. Little Rachel cried, and Samuel said, "I don't want to go." But I was determined to try. "I don't see how it can do any harm," I said. "They won't do anything worse than to send us away, and even then we should be as well off as we are now. I do so want the Master's blessing for my children!" Then one of the mothers said, "Well, if you are really going, I think I will take my children and go with you"; and at last there were three or four of us who started out with our children.

We all felt rather anxious, but I had heard so much about the Master and His loving-kindness that I felt sure He would not send us away if we could only get near enough for Him to see us. I was more afraid that the people would crowd us out.

At last we came near to the place where He was teaching, and my heart began to beat very fast. "You go first," the other mothers said; "and we will follow you." So I took Rachel's hand, and with the baby in my arms, and Samuel and John clinging to my skirts, I tried to push my way through the crowd. We succeeded in getting near enough to see the Master; and I listened very eagerly to His words, waiting for my opportunity; for I did not want to interrupt. Baby was afraid of the crowd, and began to cry; and I could not hush her. Then one of the disciples—I think his name was Peter—said to me: "What are you doing here? Don't you see that the Master is teaching and healing the older people? He mustn't be troubled with the children. Take them away; they will disturb Him."

I knew he was right, for of course the older people were more important; and I turned sorrowfully away. But the Master must have heard Baby Esther's cry, for He stopped talking, and looked at us as though He could see right into our hearts. Then He said to Peter: "Let the little children come to me. You must never forbid them to come, for of such is the kingdom of heaven."

Then He took the baby in His arms; and she patted His cheeks with her little hands, and was not a bit afraid. He drew Rachel to His side, and laid His hands on the boys' heads, and blessed them. Then He called the other mothers to Him, and He blessed us all and our children. We went away very happy, and I am sure the children will never forget Him. His blessing will always follow them, and I cannot think they will ever wilfully do anything that would grieve Him.

His words are meant just as much for children of to-day; and, if any one now should try to keep the children away from Him, I think that again they would hear His voice in their hearts saying,

"Suffer the little children to come unto me.
Forbid them not;
Of such is the kingdom of heaven."

TREASURES ON EARTH OR TREASURES IN HEAVEN

(As the story might be told)

If you and I had been in the Holy Land once upon a time, we might have seen Jesus and His disciples walking towards Jerusalem. Perhaps John would have been walking next to Jesus, and Peter and Andrew would not have been far from Him. Perhaps Peter would have been asking questions about the time when all the people would acknowledge Jesus as king. I am sure we should have joined that company, and we should have been glad to listen to every word that Jesus spoke.

Presently, as we walked and talked, we might have heard behind us the sound of running footsteps; and, as we turned to look, we should have seen a fine-looking young man, richly dressed, hurrying to catch us.

I think it would have surprised us if we could have seen him run to Jesus, and kneel down before Him, asking earnestly, "Good Master, what shall I do that I may inherit eternal life?" There had been crowds of people coming to Jesus, and many of them would have kneeled before Him, asking His help; but they would have been mostly poor people. This young man was very rich, as we could plainly see; and not many rich people had come to Jesus.

How we should have looked and listened, as the young man asked this question, and how eagerly we should have waited for the Master's answer! I think we should have been quite surprised when Jesus answered him with another question, "Why do you call me good? There is only One who is good; that is God."

The young man did not seem to know how to answer this; so he said nothing, and Jesus went on, "You know the commandments." And then He repeated four or five of the Ten Commandments, which we know as well as that young man who lived so long ago knew them. Perhaps we should have begun to ask ourselves how many of them we were keeping. I wonder whether we could honestly have answered as this young man did, "Master, I have faithfully tried all my life to keep these commandments." Then I think we should have seen a very loving look on the Master's face, and perhaps John would have whispered, "See how He loves this young man."

But Jesus could look right into the young man's

heart, just as He looks into ours; and He saw that he cared too much about money and the things money could buy. Lovingly and sorrowfully He said: "There is one thing more you must do. Go and sell what you have, and give to the poor; and come, follow me; and instead of all your riches here you shall have treasure in heaven."

That was a very hard saying, for this young man was very rich, as Jesus knew; and to sell all his property and give his money to the poor, seemed too hard, even with the promise of treasure in heaven. He wanted the treasure in heaven which Jesus was promising him, but he seemed to think the price was too high. What! give all his money to the poor, and become a poor man himself? It was too much. He felt that he could not do it, and we should have seen him go away with a sorrowful face. I think he was very unhappy with all his money, for he could not realize how much happier the treasures in heaven would have made him. Then, as we watched him slowly walking away, we should have heard Jesus say to His disciples, "How hard is it for them that trust in riches to enter into the kingdom of God!"

I am sure that, if we had been there, and had seen and heard all this, we should have learned the lesson Jesus wanted to teach, that there is no treasure on earth worth anything as compared with treasure in heaven; and we should have tried always to remember the words that He spoke at another time:

"Lay not up for yourselves treasures upon the earth, where moth and rust consume, and where thieves break through and steal; but lay up for yourselves treasures in heaven, where neither moth nor rust doth consume, and where thieves do not break through nor steal; for where thy treasure is, there will thy heart be also."

FOUR MEN WHO BROUGHT THEIR FRIEND TO JESUS

(As one of the four might have told it)

A FRIEND of ours was lying on his bed, helpless and forlorn; and we had often wished that we knew how to help him, as he would have helped us in any trouble if he could; but the poor man could not move from his bed, and there seemed to be nothing we could do for him.

One day, however, we learned to our great joy that Jesus had come to our city, and was staying in a house not far away; so four of us got together, and offered to carry our friend to Jesus that he might be healed. He did not have so much faith as we had, for he was helpless and discouraged; but he was thankful for our kindness and glad to be carried to Jesus.

We took him just as he was, on his bed, and carried him to the house where Jesus was; but we were very disappointed when we found so great a crowd already there that we could not even get near the door ourselves, to say nothing of carrying in the sick man on his bed.

Our friend was not only disappointed but discouraged, and he said, "There, I told you it was no use; we can never get near enough even to hear His words; He can't even see me; but I do almost believe He could heal me if I could only get near Him." Then we said, "Never fear; you shall get near Him; we'll manage it in some way." Then we four talked it over together, and planned what to do next. We took up his couch again, and very carefully we carried him up the outside steps to the top of the house; and, taking off some of the tiling from the roof, we made an opening big enough to let him through; and then with ropes we let him down, bed and all, right into the room, and set his bed down right before Jesus; for we believed that if Jesus saw him He would heal him.

We had already learned to believe in the Christ; and, as He looked right into our hearts and saw our faith, and saw, too, the weaker faith of the helpless man we had brought to Him, He said in a gentle voice, "Son, thy sins be forgiven thee." Our friend told us afterward that there came then a great peace into his heart, and he knew that it would be well with him whether he were healed or not, and that Jesus would do just what was best for him.

There were some Pharisees in that crowd; and I

saw them look at one another, as one of them whispered, "This man blasphemeth; no one can forgive sins but God." But Jesus knew their thoughts, just as He knows ours to-day; and He said to them, "Which do you think is easier, to say, 'Thy sins are forgiven,' or to say, 'Arise, take up thy bed, and walk'? But that you may know that the Son of man really has power to forgive sins," turning to our friend, He said, "Arise, and take up thy bed, and go thy way into thine house."

Immediately our friend stood up, and, picking up his couch as though it was a very little thing, walked away with it, thanking and praising God as he went; and the people who saw it "were all amazed, and glorified God, saying, We never saw it on this fashion."

I think we were perhaps the happiest men in Galilee that day, for we had brought our friend to Jesus, and we had learned that He cared for us and for everybody who needs His help; and from that time we lived happily, "casting all our care upon Him," for we knew that He cared for us.

JESUS IN A RICH MAN'S HOME

If we had been in a city called Jericho, in the Holy Land, many hundreds of years ago, we might have seen a great crowd of people hurrying along the city streets as fast as they could go. I think we should have hurried after them to see what was going on. Probably we should have asked the first person who could stop to listen to us what had happened and where all the people were going in such a hurry. Perhaps his answer would have been something like this: "Why, haven't you heard that Jesus of Nazareth is coming to our town? I suppose He will stay all night, and I am wondering in whose home He will stay. I wish I could invite Him to our house, but I'm afraid we haven't room enough."

I think that by this time we should all have been very much excited, and should have hurried down the street with the crowd. As we went, we might have seen a little man before us, such a very little man that perhaps we should have smiled as we watched him hurrying along; and we might have said, "I'm afraid the little man won't get a chance to see much in this crowd."

Then, as we watched, we should have seen him suddenly edge away from the crowd, and climb up into a tree that stood by the roadside; and perhaps some boy in the crowd would have said, "He is going to see all there is to be seen, after all." It may be that we should have heard some of the people jeering and laughing at him, as they said: "Just look at little old Zacchæus climbing up into that tree! What good does he expect to get from this visit of Jesus? I should think he would be ashamed to look at Him. The old cheat!" Perhaps we should have asked some one to tell us why they disliked the little man so, and the answer might have been, "O, he is a publican; he collects taxes from us all for the Romans. No one likes the publicans; they are all cheats and rogues, we say."

By this time Jesus would have been very near, and there would be no time for talking, for I am sure we should all have felt very much as Zacchæus did, that we must see Jesus. How surprised we should have been, when the crowd came near to the sycamore-tree, and Jesus suddenly stopped and called out in a loud, clear voice, "Zacchæus, make haste, and come down, for to-day I must abide at thy house"! O, how surprised and pleased Zacchæus must have been! I believe that he came down from that tree much more quickly than he went up, and I am sure he gave Jesus a joyful welcome. He would never have said, "We haven't room enough." There would surely have been room for Jesus in his home, whoever else might be there.

Perhaps just then we might have seen the man who had wished Jesus could come to his house, only he had no room for Him; and we might have heard him say: "Well, what a strange thing to do! Why, he is gone in to lodge with a man that is a sinner! That is the last place I should have expected Him to visit. I wonder whether He knows what sort of a man Zacchæus is." How we should have listened to what Zacchæus would say, and what Jesus would say!

Then we might have seen little Zacchæus stand forth in the sight of all the people, and say in a loud voice, "Behold, Lord, the half of my goods I now give to the poor; and, if I have wronged any man, I will give him back four times as much." I think some of the people would have looked a little ashamed as they heard Jesus say something like this: "This day is salvation come to this house. The Son of man came to seek and to save that which is lost. If Zacchæus is such a sinner as you say, then he is the very man I came to save.''

I wonder whether we should have stood with the crowd, watching Him in silence as He walked home with Zacchæus, or should we have followed Jesus and asked whether we too might go to Zacchæus's home, and listen to His words? I wonder whether we are trying now to be like Zacchæus, hurrying to see Jesus, welcoming Him to our hearts and homes, and trying so far as we can to undo all the wrong things we have done, and to do what will please Jesus. We can come to Jesus to-day just as truly as Zacchæus did, and Jesus will be just as glad to visit us as He was to visit Zacchæus if we can sing from our hearts the words,

"O, come to my heart, Lord Jesus, come;
There is room in my heart for Thee."

THE STORY OF A MAN WHO BOASTED

(As Peter might have told it)

It was the very last night that our Lord was with us on earth that I so grieved His heart by boasting. We had eaten the passover supper; and He had told us to observe this supper in remembrance of Him, as He broke the bread and blessed it, and passed to us the cup, saying, "Drink ye all of it"; and then He said, "Verily I say unto you, I shall no more drink of the fruit of the vine until that day when I drink it new in the kingdom of God."

I remember how lovingly yet sorrowfully the Master looked into our faces as He said, "A new commandment I give unto you, that ye love one another as I have loved you."

I am sure we were all ashamed of ourselves then, for we had not been very loving when we had quarrelled as to who should be greatest in His kingdom. I remember it all so distinctly now, but just then I was not thinking what He was saying, for I was puzzling about something He had said a few moments ago about going somewhere where

THE STORY OF A MAN WHO BOASTED 147

we could not follow Him. Now I felt so sure that I would go wherever He could that I said, "Lord, whither goest Thou?"

He looked at me kindly, and said, "Whither I go thou canst not follow me now, but thou shalt follow me afterward."

But I answered: "Lord, why cannot I follow Thee now? I am ready to go with Thee both into prison and to death."

And then the Master answered sadly, "I tell thee, Peter, that this day, even in this night, before the cock crow twice, thou shalt deny me thrice."

But I was so proud and so sure of myself that again I boasted, "Though I should die with Thee, yet will I not deny Thee," I said.

I think it was because I felt so sure of myself, and because I boasted, that I failed Him so quickly; for ever since that day I have known that the man who boasts forgets God, and is very likely to sin just because he does not watch against temptation.

It all happened just as He had said, that very same evening; for when, a little later, in the Garden of Gethsemane, the Roman guard came to arrest Him, we all forsook Him and fled; and I, who had boasted so great things, was the very worst of all: for I did say three times that very night that

I did not know Him and had never been one of His disciples, and all because I was afraid to follow Him to death as I had boasted that I would. It was only when I heard the cock crowing in the early morning, and saw Him turn and look at me, that I remembered His words; and, though I went out and wept bitterly, and though I did truly repent of my sin, yet I could not undo it. I had boasted that I would be true though every one else should fail Him, and then I had denied that I knew Him!

I am glad to remember that He did forgive me afterward, and I tried always to be faithful to Him from that time. Later I did follow in His steps even to prison, for the Jews imprisoned me for teaching in His name; and it may be that sometime I shall have to follow Him even to death; but, if that must be, I hope I shall be found faithful, for I have learned my lesson; and now I often say to myself, "Let him that thinketh he standeth take heed lest he fall"; and I do not boast any more of what I will do.

THE STORY OF A MAN WHO WAS AFRAID TO DO RIGHT

(As Pilate himself might tell it if he could come back)

I WAS the Roman governor in Jerusalem, Cæsar's representative; the supreme power of the province was in my hands. I was glad to be in command; and yet it was not altogether a desirable position, for the Jews were not easy to govern. They hated the Romans, and they hated me; and, indeed, I hated them too, because they had so often rebelled against my authority, and threatened to complain of me to Cæsar, and, if possible, have me removed from my high position as governor.

Yet among all the difficulties and troubles that I had had there was nothing that so perplexed and troubled me as the case of Jesus of Nazareth, the "King of the Jews," as many called Him, though I had never heard of His calling Himself by that title. I had watched Him and spied upon Him, but I had never heard anything evil concerning Him; and when, very early one morning, the rulers of the Jews led Him to my judgment-seat, demanding that He be put to death, I did not know what to do. I *ought* to have known, for I believed Him to be innocent, and I was sure that they could not prove their charges against Him; but I was afraid to do right.

I asked them what accusation they had brought against Him, and they said: "If He were not a wicked man who deserved to die, we would not have brought Him before thee. We found this fellow perverting the people, and forbidding them to give tribute to Cæsar, saying that He Himself is Christ, a king, and the Son of God."

When I heard that, I was afraid; for it seemed to me, from all I had seen and heard of Him, that He might really be the Son of God. I did not for a moment believe that their accusation was true, but I took the prisoner one side, and questioned Him alone; and then I was even more afraid, for I found no fault in Him, and I did not know what to do. While I was thinking about it with a troubled heart, this message was brought to me from one in my home: "Have nothing to do with that righteous man, for I have suffered many things this day in a dream because of Him." I knew that this advice was good, and I wished that I need have nothing to do with "that righteous

A MAN AFRAID TO DO RIGHT 151

man"; but how should I get rid of the case? I was afraid of Him, and I was afraid of the people.

I sent Him to Herod, hoping that he would dispose of the business; but Herod found no fault in Him, and sent Him back to me. I tried in every way I could think of to persuade the people to let me release Him; but they said, "If thou let this man go, thou art not Cæsar's friend; for whosoever maketh himself a king speaketh against Cæsar." Then I offered to admit that He was guilty, but I would set Him free, as it was my custom always to release one prisoner at passover-time, and this time it should be Jesus Christ. When they still protested, I gave them their choice; I would release Jesus or Barabbas, a man who was a notable robber and murderer, and of whom every one was afraid; but they all cried out with one voice that I should release Barabbas, and that Jesus should be crucified.

I knew it was a wrong and wicked thing to do, but I yielded to them because I was afraid to do the right thing. If they should accuse me to Cæsar, as they threatened, I should lose my position; and so for fear of the Jews I yielded and did what I knew was wicked; I washed my hands before them all, and told them I would wash away this guilt from my hands, and the sin was theirs;

and then I delivered Jesus to them to be crucified, saying that it was their fault and not mine. But all the time I knew that it really was my fault, and that I could not wash my hands of it; I knew in my inmost soul that I was really the one who crucified Jesus.

I know now, and I think I really knew even then, that nothing they could do to me, even if they did their worst, would be so hard to bear, as the accusations of my own conscience would be if I should do that wicked thing; but because I was afraid I did it. Oh, how I suffered for it all the rest of my life! and how often I wished that I had been able to say, as did one of their own writers, "In God have I put my trust; I will not be afraid what man can do unto me."

TWO MEN WHO TOOK A WALK WITH JESUS

(*A Word Picture*)

ONCE upon a time, away back in the long ago, in a country far, far away, I seem to see two men walking and talking together one afternoon near the setting of the sun. They were not happy men, one could see; for their faces were sad and their voices were sorrowful. We do not know exactly what they were saying, but we can imagine that it was something like this:

"When did you first see Him?" Cleopas would say.

"O, a long time ago," the other might answer; "it was that day on the mountain when He talked about the laws of the kingdom, and taught us how to pray, and told the story of the two men who built their houses, one on the sand, and one on the rock."

"O, yes, I heard that," Cleopas would say, "and don't you remember how He said that, if we heard those sayings of His, and did those things which

He taught, our houses were founded upon the rock? His teachings were good, and His deeds were good; but I am afraid we were mistaken in Him, after all. I thought He was 'the Coming One'; but they have killed Him, and that is the end of our hopes.''

"I am afraid so," the other would answer; "and yet, when I remember all the wonderful things that He said and did, it seems as though He must have been what He claimed. Were you there when He raised Lazarus from the dead?"

"Yes, I was there; and I have seen Him do many other wonderful works, and He spake as never man spake. O, how could they do it? Why did He let them kill Him? He saved others; surely He could have saved Himself."

"But what do you think of that story those women told us this morning about seeing some angels who told them that He was alive?" the other might ask.

"O, they must have been mistaken," Cleopas would answer. "You know Peter went himself to the sepulchre; it is true that he found it empty as the women said, but he did not see Jesus."

"Well, it is all very hard to understand," the other would answer; "I did so hope it was all true."

We can almost see these two men walking so sadly along the road on their way to their home in Emmaus, on the third day after Jesus was crucified; and we can seem to hear their very words as they talk of all the things that have happened in Jerusalem in these last three days. But now, as we look at them and listen to their words, One is coming to join them in their walk; and our own hearts seem to burn within us as we listen while He asks them what they are talking about and why they are so sad. What do you suppose we should say if some day Jesus should join us in our walk, and ask us what we were talking about? O, I hope He would not hear any of us saying anything unkind or untrue, or anything that would grieve Him; but we must not forget that He is with us every day in all our walks and talks, though we do not see Him.

Cleopas told Him of their talk, and we can see His wonderful look of loving-kindness as He tells them how foolish and slow of heart they have been that they have not understood their Bible; for then they would have known that all this must happen, and they would have believed the story the women had told that very morning of their vision of angels. How their hearts burned within them as they listened, while He opened to them the

Scriptures and explained what the prophets had written! How firmly they believed it all now, and how foolish they felt themselves to have been not to have so studied their Bible that they would have understood it all beforehand!

But now, if you look into the sky, you will see that it is almost sunset, and they are drawing near to their home; and, though they do not seem to know who this stranger is, yet they do not want to lose His company. Can't you hear them asking Him to come in and stay with them? I wonder how often we have asked Him to come in and stay in our homes; I am sure that He is just as ready to come now as then.

And now I wonder whether your imagination is so strong that you can see the three at their evening meal, and can hear the Stranger as He asks the blessing. Do you think of Him sometimes when the blessing is asked at your table? And now, see what a wonderful thing is happening! As He speaks, all at once they know it is Jesus; and in that moment He vanishes from their sight.

Now what do you think they will do next? Will they sit down and talk it all over as they eat their evening meal? Not they! I don't believe that meal was ever eaten; for I seem to see them now, hurrying back to Jerusalem, talking eagerly as they go, trying to remember every single word that Jesus spoke to them.

And here they are, back in Jerusalem again, in that upper chamber where the eleven are gathered, all eagerly talking. Can you hear what John is saying as they enter the room? "The Lord is risen indeed, and hath appeared to Simon!" he says. Aren't you glad that He appeared to Peter so soon? It must have been then, I think, that Peter knew that he was forgiven. And now the two are talking, and they will not stop until they have "told what things were done in the way," and how the Lord was known of them in breaking of bread and blessing it. Aren't you glad they have told the rest all they knew about Jesus their Saviour, and don't you suppose that is what Jesus wants us to do, that we also may help others to believe in Him?

WHAT HAPPENED TO A CRIPPLE

(As the cripple himself might have told the story)

I HAD never known what it was to be well. From my very babyhood I had always been a cripple, and had had to be carried everywhere. As soon as I was old enough, I had to get my own living as best I could; and the only way I knew of getting it was to beg. Every morning I used to get some one to carry me from my home, and lay me down beside that gate of the temple which we called Beautiful.

I felt that the people who went through that gate and into the temple to worship God would be the ones who would be most likely to help me, because they would be the people who would remember the words that God had spoken through His servant Moses, "If there be among you a poor man of one of thy brethren within any of thy gates in thy land which the Lord thy God giveth thee, thou shalt not harden thine heart, nor shut thine hand from thy poor brother; but thou shalt open thine hand wide unto him."

Then, too, I had heard of Jesus, though I had

WHAT HAPPENED TO A CRIPPLE 159

never seen Him; and some one had told me that He had once said to His disciples, "Freely ye have received; freely give"; so I felt sure that here at the Beautiful Gate I should find those who would help me.

I was now forty years old, and all those forty years I had been a cripple. Every day I had been carried to the temple, and many had hardened their hearts and passed me by without even looking; but some had helped.

One day, as I was lying there, I saw two men coming up to the temple who looked different from the rest; they had so pleasant, kind faces! One was a young man, and the other much older; but they seemed to be great friends, and they looked as though they would be friendly with everybody.

I asked them for money, and I felt sure they would give me something. They stopped instantly, and the older man, looking at me very earnestly, said, "Look on us." I looked eagerly, believing that they would surely give me money; but the older man, whose name I afterward learned was Peter, said, "I haven't any silver or gold, but such as I have I will give"; and then, with a very earnest and solemn voice he said, "In the name of Jesus Christ of Nazareth, rise up and walk!"

Immediately I felt that I could do it, though I

had never walked a step in my life. He took me by the hand, and God gave me strength to stand up and walk. O, I don't believe you can half know how thankful I was! I jumped; I ran; I stood still; I walked; and all the time I was praising and thanking God with a loud voice for all His goodness to me; and all the people heard me.

Of course I walked into the temple first of all; for I wanted to thank God in His house, and I wanted everybody to know that I was thanking Him. It seemed as though I could never thank Him enough, and in all my after-life I tried to show my thankfulness by telling others how I had been healed through the power of Jesus Christ. Often, as I went to the temple, I used to sing the words of one of our Psalms,

> "Enter into His gates with thanksgiving,
> And into His courts with praise;
> Be thankful unto Him,
> And bless His name."

It did me good to say "Thank you" to God, and I believe it was also good for those who heard me, and I know the Psalmist was right when he said,

> "It is a good thing to give thanks
> Unto the Lord,
> And to sing praises unto Thy name,
> O Most High."

A WOMAN WHO PRETENDED TO BE GOOD

(As Sapphira might tell it now if she could come back)

I WAS a wicked woman, and I knew it, and I was as much to blame as Ananias. We were counted among the followers of Jesus, and in a general way we meant to do what was right; but sometimes it seemed to us that the apostles asked too much of us. And when it came to pass that all the Christians began to sell their possessions, and give their money into the general fund for the good of all, we did not want to do as they were doing.

We thought we should feel rather ashamed not to do what the others did, and we did not want them to think us mean and selfish; yet we could not quite make up our minds to give away so much money. We talked it over together many times, and at last we made a plan. We would sell our land, and hand over a part of the money to the apostles for the general fund; and the rest we would keep for ourselves. We knew that the others were giving all; but we would not tell them how much we sold the land for, and they would think that of course we had given it all. We need not say anything about the price we had received, but just go forward with the others and hand over the money; and they would take it for granted that we had given all, and would think we were generous.

Of course we were not obliged to sell the land, or to give away any of the money; but we wanted to be thought as kind and generous as other people. I am afraid we cared more for what men thought of us than for what God thought.

Well, we did just as we had planned. We sold our land, and Ananias carried part of the money to Peter. I waited anxiously at home for Ananias to come back; for I wanted to know what Peter would say, and whether others would praise us for our generosity. I waited and waited and waited a long time; but Ananias did not come back, and I could not think what had become of him.

At last I could not bear it any longer, and I decided that I too would go to Peter and find out what he had said, and why Ananias had not come back. I did not find Ananias; and, when I spoke to Peter about the money, he asked me at once, "Did you sell the land for just so much?" And I could not stop to think; so I said, "Yes, for so much." Until now my sin had been selfishness

A WOMAN PRETENDED TO BE GOOD 163

and trying to seem better than I was; but now I had added another sin to cover up the first ones, for I had told a lie.

Then Peter told me, as he had already told Ananias, that we had not lied unto men, but unto God, and that I must die for my sins as Ananias had already died; and, as he spoke the words, I fell at his feet dead.

O, if I could go back now to the people who live on the earth, I would say to them, "Do not try to seem good in the sight of men, but rather ' study to show yourselves approved unto God.' When you come to die, you will not care so much what men think of you, but you will care very much what God thinks of you. Be honest and true, and try always to do what is right in God's sight. If you have not always done this, ask God to forgive you, and begin all over again now, and try always to be what you seem, and to do right in God's sight. I wish I had always remembered what God once said to Samuel:

" 'The Lord seeth not as man seeth;
Man looketh on the outward appearance.
The Lord looketh on the heart.' "

DORCAS, THE FRIEND OF THE POOR

(As one of her neighbors might have told the story afterward)

I WAS a woman who lived long ago in Joppa. My nearest neighbor was a woman named Dorcas, and she lived so beautiful, kindly a life that she helped all her neighbors to be more kind and thoughtful for others, though she never said much to us about being good, or caring for the poor, or trying to please God.

I often wondered how she could be so forgetful of herself and so thoughtful for others; for she was always doing kind things for some one. I often thought as I watched her daily life of the words that our Master once spoke, "Inasmuch as ye have done it unto one of the least of these my brethren, ye have done it unto me." I am sure that, if she had ever seen the Master in need of food or clothing, she would have ministered to Him; and it must have been a joy to her to think that in caring for His children she was ministering to Him.

If any of the neighbors were sick, they always sent for her; if any one was suffering, she seemed to know of it without being told; and she always carried help and comfort wherever there was

DORCAS, THE FRIEND OF THE POOR

trouble. If her neighbors were joyful and happy, she rejoiced with them; and, if they were unhappy, she comforted them. We used to say of her that she was "full of good works." She often made me think of what the wise man once wrote, "She openeth her mouth with wisdom, and in her tongue is the law of kindness."

In her spare time she was always sewing for the poor, and many were the little coats and dresses that she made for those who were in need. I often used to meet poor people, sometimes widows and sometimes little children, wearing clothes that I knew she had made for them.

One day I went to see her, expecting to find her sewing as usual; but I was sorry to find that she was very sick. She did not complain, but only said that she was sorry she had not been able to finish the little coat that she was making for a neighbor's little boy who needed it very much.

She died a few days later, and there was great sorrow in Joppa when people heard of her death. There were a good many Christians in that city, and one of them suggested that we should send for Peter, who was staying at Lydda, a town not far away. So we sent two men with an urgent message, asking him to come to us at once; and he came hurrying back with them.

We told him all about Dorcas, and our great sorrow, and what a loss it was to all the poor people of the neighborhood. We did not suppose that he could do anything, but it was a comfort to tell him all about it.

We took him to the home of Dorcas; and, when we went up-stairs, we found in her room a great company of women, among them many widows that she had helped; and they were all crying, and showing the coats and garments that she had made while she was with us. One woman said, "Look! she made this dress that I have on." Another said, "See my little boy; she made the coat he is wearing." There was hardly any one in the room who had not received some kindness from her, and we did not wonder that they were crying.

But Peter asked them all to go out of the room, and then he kneeled down and prayed. He must have had great faith; for, as he prayed he felt that his prayer was answered, and, turning to the bed, he said, "Tabitha," for that was her other name, "Tabitha, arise!" And immediately she opened her eyes; and, when she saw Peter, she sat up. "And he gave her his hand, and lifted her up; and, when he had called the saints and widows, presented her alive. And it was known throughout all Joppa, and many believed in the Lord."

HOW PAUL CONFESSED CHRIST ON THE DAMASCUS ROAD

(As Paul himself might have told the story)

THERE was a time when I distinctly chose not to confess Christ, and not only that, but I determined that, so far as I could prevent it, no one else should confess Him; and so I persecuted His followers everywhere.

But there came a time when Christ revealed Himself to me in a wonderful manner. I was on my way to Damascus to persecute the Christians there, when suddenly there shone from heaven a great light round about me. I fell to the ground, and I heard Christ's voice, as He told me that in persecuting His followers I was persecuting Him. At that very instant I faced right about, and chose to become His follower instead of His persecutor; and I said, "What wilt Thou have me to do, Lord?" I felt at once that I wanted to do His will and not my own. He told me to arise and go into the city, and there I should be told what I was to do.

When I arose, I could not see anything, for the light had blinded me; but the soldiers who were with me led me by the hand, and took me to the home of Judas; and there I stayed for three days, not able to see anything or to eat anything. All the time I was just thinking, thinking, thinking; and, when I was not thinking I was praying, praying, praying, for I knew there must be a great change in my life after this, and I longed for guidance and wisdom to know how I might best serve the Lord Christ, whom at last I knew and loved.

After a few days, Ananias, one of the Christians who lived in Damascus, came to me, and stood by me, and said, "Brother Saul, receive thy sight. God has chosen thee to be His witness unto all men." I was greatly surprised that one of the very men I had meant to persecute should be willing to call me "brother"; and it was Ananias, now my friend, who gave me my first lesson in the Christian life.

As soon as I could I went away into Arabia, that I might be alone to think and pray and plan. After my stay in the desert of Arabia I went right back to Damascus, that I might confess Christ as my Master there in the very city where I had meant to deny Him and to persecute His followers. Publicly in their synagogues I confessed

HOW PAUL CONFESSED CHRIST 169

Christ, saying to every one, "He is the Son of God." I knew that this public confession of Christ would bring me into danger, but I was so glad to be counted as His follower that I wanted every one to know it, and I wanted to bring as many others as I could into the joy of that discipleship.

It was not long before the Jews, who would not accept Christ as their Lord, and would not let others confess Him, began to plot how they might kill me, even as I had planned to kill others; but some of the Christians, who called themselves my brethren now, helped me to escape, letting me down from a window in the wall, in a basket on a dark night; and so I was safe for that time.

After that it was always a joy to me to confess Christ whenever and wherever I had opportunity, though often it cost me much suffering, and often it led me into great danger; but always I could rejoice in my Master's words, "Whosoever shall confess me before men, him will I confess also before my Father which is in heaven."

I suppose no one was ever led to make his first confession of Christ in so wonderful a way as I was, for all people are led to Him in different ways; but all may come to Him, and all may know the joy of confession, and may know that Christ will always own as His children those who own Him as their Lord and Master. We should always be very, very glad to make it known that we belong to Him.

A STORY OF "A HELPER OF MANY"

(As Phœbe might have told it)

My home was in Cenchreæ, one of the ports of the great city of Corinth; and ever since I had learned from Paul what it meant to be a follower of Jesus I had tried to do what I could to help others to know God's law and obey it. I was a member of the church that was in Cenchreæ, and I had tried, so far as I could, to help in all the work of that church. But the time came when I must leave my home and take the long journey to Rome. When Paul heard that I was going there, he said that he would like to send a letter by me to the Christians in Rome; and Tertius, who had the pen of a ready writer, promised to write it at Paul's dictation.

Paul had never been in Rome, but he had long been planning to go there when there should be an opportunity. Alas! that opportunity never came to him till he went there as a prisoner, falsely accused by the very people he was trying to help.

There were a good many Christians in Rome, a few of them friends of Paul's; and others, I suppose, had heard the story of Jesus and His love from some of the apostles, when they had sometimes been to Jerusalem to attend a feast. I knew they would be very glad to get Paul's letter; and I felt very much honored to think that he would trust me to carry it, and that he even mentioned my name in it, and recommended me to his friends in Rome.

It was a long, hard journey, and sometimes a dangerous one. I felt very anxious lest I should fail to get safely to Rome with the precious letter; but Paul dictated it, and Tertius wrote it for him. Then he copied it off carefully, and first of all read it aloud to the church in Corinth; and then he wrapped it up in many wrappings and gave it to me, and I started on my journey.

I was very glad when at last the long voyage was over, and I arrived safely in Rome, and handed the letter to the elders of the church; and very eagerly I listened again to Paul's words, as it was read aloud to the Christians who had gathered to hear it.

He told them in this letter that their faith was known throughout the Roman Empire, and that he very much desired to preach the gospel to the Christians in Rome. He told them of the power of the gospel of Christ, and how from the beginning

A STORY OF "A HELPER OF MANY" 173

of the world God had revealed Himself to the hearts of men; but they had made idols, and had worshipped them, as many Romans did still. He reminded them that the old way of trying to be righteous by keeping the Jewish law had passed away, and that the new way of righteousness by faith in Jesus had come. Then, after writing more advice, especially for the Jews, he added some counsels for all Christians of whatever race or language.

He gave them many simple rules for Christian living, such as you have read in your Bible in Romans 12: 9-21, and then he closed with special personal greetings to all his friends in Rome.

I felt very glad and very humble, as they read what he had said of me. "I commend unto you Phœbe, our sister," he wrote, "who is a servant of the church which is at Cenchreæ; that ye receive her in the Lord, worthily of the saints, and that ye assist her in whatsoever matter she may have need of you; for she herself also hath been a helper of many, and of mine own self."

I do so like the title he gave me, "**a helper of many**"; and I have tried ever since then to deserve it. That is what I want to be always, "Phœbe the helper," and I am sure God wants us all to be "helpers of many."

PAUL'S HELPERS AND HINDERERS

(As Paul might have told the story)

My life was a very busy one, with many troubles and trials and many joys; and most of my joys and trials I owed to my helpers and hinderers.

I was a hinderer myself at first, for I persecuted the Christians unto death, "binding and delivering into prisons both men and women." But my Lord met me on the Damascus road, and showed me how wrong I was; and from that time I was a changed man, and instead of being a hinderer I began to be a helper.

There were many people after that who tried to hinder me, but I found my first helper right there in Damascus. There was a man in that city named Ananias, who was almost afraid to come near me, because he knew how I had persecuted the Christians; yet he bravely came to my help, and brought me a message from my Lord; and through his help my sight was given back to me, for I had been blind ever since my vision of the Christ on the Damascus road. I can never forget what Ananias did for me, though I was never able to see much of him afterward.

PAUL'S HELPERS AND HINDERERS 175

There were other friends in Damascus, too; and they came to my rescue when my would-be hinderers were seeking to kill me. These kind friends warned me of my danger, and led me to the house of a friendly Christian, whose house was on the city wall; and they let me down in a basket in the night; and so I escaped from the city and from my enemies.

When later I went to Jerusalem to try to undo, so far as I could, the evil I had done there, the disciples were all afraid of me. I could not blame them since I had once been such a hinderer; but I wished they would let me be a helper now. Then came my friend Barnabas, a kindly, gentle man, a gentleman in every sense of the word; and he went with me to the disciples, and told them that I had become a different man, and that I now preached the faith which once I tried to destroy, and they might trust me.

It was not long before there were many in Jerusalem who wished to hinder my work, and planned to kill me; but again my friends and helpers came to my rescue, and went with me as far as Cæsarea, and saw me safely on board a ship for Tarsus, my old home. I was sorry to go, for I wanted to work for Christ right there where I had worked against Him; but, if it had not been for my helpers, I should have lost my life, and should have had no opportunity to serve Him anywhere.

I cannot tell you now of all my other friends and helpers, for there were many of them. There was Phœbe, who was "a helper of many" and of myself also. Whenever I sailed from the port of Cenchreæ, her home was always my stopping-place on the way. It was Phœbe, too, who carried my letter to the Christians in Rome, a letter which is still read by Christians in every land, though I wrote it nearly two thousand years ago. I wonder whether you have read it, and whether it has helped you, for I hoped my letters would be helpful to all who should read them.

Then there was Lydia, who opened her home to me in Philippi and who dressed my wounds, and cheered and comforted me after I had been beaten and imprisoned.

There were Priscilla and Aquila, too, my friends in Corinth and Ephesus, "who for my life laid down their own necks." Then there were Luke, my beloved doctor, and Timothy and Silas, and so many others that I cannot even name them now; but I know that their names are written in God's book, and I know that whatever good work I was able to do I owed largely to them; so I like to remember the helpers and forget the hinderers.

I wonder whether you are all trying to be helpers too. Read the twelfth chapter of my letter that Phœbe carried to Rome, and that will show you some ways of helping; and then we must always remember that we can all help together by prayer.

HOW TWO MEN TURNED THE WORLD UPSIDE DOWN

(As Silas might tell the story if he could come back)

My name is Silas, and I was chosen by Paul to go with him on his second missionary journey. I don't suppose my name would ever have been heard of if it had not been for my friendship with Paul and for his great missionary work in which I tried to help him.

We had had to bear a good many hard things on our journey, especially in Philippi, where they had beaten us and put us in prison for preaching about Jesus Christ, and we had had a long, hard journey from there to Thessalonica. This was a very important seaport, and there were many travellers passing through the city in every direction; so Paul thought it was just the place for us; for, if we could persuade the Thessalonians to become followers of Christ, they would pass on the story of Jesus and His love to many others.

The people of Thessalonica were mostly Jews and Greeks; and, though the Jews believed on God,

TURNING THE WORLD UPSIDE DOWN 179

they did not know Jesus, and the Greeks worshipped idols. For three Sundays we went to the Jewish synagogue, and Paul preached to them about Jesus, explaining the Old Testament prophecies about Him, and telling them how He had died for us, that we might be saved. The people listened with great interest, and a good many of the Greeks believed Paul's teachings, and gave up their idols for the living God. But many of the Jews were envious of Paul's influence, and would not listen to his teachings, or allow others to listen if they could help it; and they soon made a great tumult in the city.

One night a mob gathered in the streets, and tried to break into the house of Jason, who was our friend, that they might take Paul and kill him. But Jason found a way to get us quietly out of the city, and sent us with friends to Berea.

I suppose you never saw such an angry crowd of people as those who were in Jason's street that night. They broke into the house, shouting and howling, and dragged Jason and some of his friends before the rulers of the city, and said, "These that have turned the world upside down have come here also." That was all they could think of to say against us, and their charge was really true, for that was just what we were trying to do. We were trying to turn the world upside down by putting down the evil and lifting up the good. The rulers were a good deal troubled and worried, but they could not find Paul; and there seemed to be nothing they could do but to bind Jason and his friends to keep the peace, and let them go.

They had driven us out of the city, but they could not drive out the effects of Paul's preaching, and we left many Christians there, though there was not one when we entered the city. If turning the world upside down means driving out the evil and bringing in the good, then we two unknown travellers had certainly turned a large part of that city upside down.

It was a great sorrow to Paul that he had to leave Thessalonica before he had finished his work there, and he longed to go back and explain to them the way of God more perfectly, but since he could not do that he wrote them a letter from Corinth some time later, making more clear to them some things that they had not understood.

In that letter he told them how glad he was that they had turned from idols "to serve the living and true God." He had heard three things about them that made him very happy, for he had heard of their "work of faith, and labor of love, and patience of hope in our Lord Jesus Christ''; and, when he thought of these things, he did not wonder that their example had been a help to Christians everywhere. "From you," he wrote, "has sounded out the word of the Lord, not only in Macedonia and Achaia, but also in every place your faith in God has gone forth."

These Thessalonians, too, were "turning the world upside down," so that not only in their own city but in many other places in all the region round about people were turning from idols to serve the living and true God. I was always glad that I went with Paul on that journey, and helped in the good work; and what Paul did I believe every one can help to do, for every one who is trying to put down the evil and lift up the good is helping at least a little to turn the world upside down as Paul did.

A LETTER PAUL WROTE ABOUT "ENDURING HARDNESS"

(*As Timothy might tell the story now*)

I WAS a very young man, not much more than a boy, when Paul and Barnabas first came to Lystra, where my home was. My father was a Greek; but my mother was a Jewess, and she and my grandmother had taught me my Bible almost from the time when I was a baby. Of course I had only the Old Testament, for the New Testament was not written then; but I knew my Bible well, and I loved God and tried to do right. I have always been glad to remember that a part of the New Testament was written specially for me. I don't suppose Paul ever thought that you would read it, or perhaps any one but myself; and yet the advice it gives is good and helpful to everybody who reads it to-day.

When Paul and Barnabas came to Lystra, I was very much interested in their teachings, for that was the first time I had heard about Jesus. Soon after they came a wonderful thing happened. There was a poor cripple sitting by the wayside begging, who had never been able to walk a step in his whole life. Paul had seen this poor lame man sitting there, and had noticed that he listened earnestly to his teachings; and, believing that he had faith to be made whole, he said in a loud voice, "Stand upright on thy feet!" And instantly he stood up and walked. The people of Lystra were so awed by what had happened that they believed Paul must be a god, and they made ready to worship him in their own fashion. I was standing by when they brought oxen and garlands to sacrifice to him; and I heard Paul say most earnestly that he was not a god, but only a man like themselves; and he urged them to worship "the living God, who made the heaven, and the earth, and the sea, and all that in them is."

From that time I took every opportunity to listen to Paul as he tried to teach the people a better way, and he taught me to believe in the Lord Jesus Christ. When later some of the Jews who hated Paul had persuaded the people to stone him, and when they drew him out of the city, and left him for dead, I was one of those who helped him to rise; and it was to my home that he was taken for rest and loving care after enduring such hardships.

When he came again to Lystra on his second

missionary journey, and invited me to travel with him and Silas, I was very glad to go, and glad that my neighbors could speak well of me so that he wanted me. Together we endured hardness many times, for I was with him in many journeys from this time till near the end of his life.

Paul's very last letter was written to me from his prison in Rome, while I was trying to help the people of Ephesus to know the Christ and obey His teachings. That last letter of his, written from a Roman prison, has been a great comfort and help, not only to me, but to thousands of Christians ever since.

He knew that in Ephesus, where most of the people worshipped the goddess Diana in the great temple that was one of the seven wonders of the world, I should have many hard things to bear; and he wanted to strengthen me to bear them. He was himself enduring hardness while he wrote, but he was bearing it cheerily, and he told me that I must take my part in enduring hardness. He said I must not have a spirit of fearfulness, but of power and love. It was because he had been preaching Christ Jesus that he was now enduring hardship in prison; but he said, "I am not ashamed, for I know Him whom I have believed, and am persuaded that He is able to guard that which I have committed unto Him." Then he added, "Thou, therefore, my son, be strong in the grace that is in Christ Jesus. . . . Endure hardness, as a good soldier of Jesus Christ, and try to please Him who hath chosen you to be a soldier."

That is the way we can all endure hardness, by trying to please Him who has chosen us to be His soldiers; and He will make us strong. I had many hard things to bear in Ephesus for many years after Paul died; but I had his precious letter, and that always helped me, as I believe it will help you. "Trusting in the Lord Jesus Christ for strength," we can all learn to endure hardness, and so become "strong in the Lord, and in the power of His might."